The Eiffel Tower and Other Mythologies

Copyright © 1979 by Farrar, Straus and Giroux, Inc.
All rights reserved
First American edition, 1979
Published simultaneously in Canada
by McGraw-Hill Ryerson Ltd., Toronto
Printed in the United States of America
Designed by Jeffrey Schaire

Library of Congress Cataloging in Publication Data
Barthes, Roland.
The Eiffel Tower, and other mythologies.
I. Title.
AC8.B4353   1979   081   79-15692

"The Eiffel Tower" is translated from La Tour Eiffel. "Buffet donne le
coup de grâce à New York" first appeared in the French Arts; and "Les
deux salons," "Wagon-restaurant," and "Tricots à domicile" in Les Let-
tres Nouvelles. The other essays are translated from the French Mythologies.

THE EIFFEL TOWER

and Other Mythologies

ROLAND BARTHES

Translated by Richard Howard

HILL AND WANG
NEW YORK
A division of Farrar, Straus and Giroux

Contents

The Eiffel Tower and Other Mythologies

The
Eiffel
Tower

MAUPASSANT OFTEN LUNCHED AT THE RES-
taurant in the tower, though he didn't care much for
the food: *It's the only place in Paris,* he used to say, *where I
don't have to see it.* And it's true that you must take endless
precautions, in Paris, not to see the Eiffel Tower; whatever
the season, through mist and cloud, on overcast days or in
sunshine, in rain—wherever you are, whatever the landscape
of roofs, domes, or branches separating you from it, *the
Tower is there;* incorporated into daily life until you can no
longer grant it any specific attribute, determined merely to
persist, like a rock or the river, it is as literal as a phenomenon
of nature whose meaning can be questioned to infinity but
whose existence is incontestable. There is virtually no Parisian glance it fails to *touch* at some time of day; at the
moment I begin writing these lines about it, the Tower is
there, in front of me, framed by my window; and at the very
moment the January night blurs it, apparently trying to make
it invisible, to deny its presence, two little lights come on,
winking gently as they revolve at its very tip: all this night,
too, it will be there, connecting me above Paris to each of my
friends that I know are seeing it: with it we all comprise a
shifting figure of which it is the steady center: the Tower is
friendly.

The Tower is also present to the entire world. First of all
as a universal symbol of Paris, it is everywhere on the globe
where Paris is to be stated as an image; from the Midwest to
Australia, there is no journey to France which isn't made,

3

somehow, in the Tower's name, no schoolbook, poster, or film about France which fails to propose it as the major sign of a people and of a place: it belongs to the universal language of travel. Further: beyond its strictly Parisian statement, it touches the most general human image-repertoire: its simple, primary shape confers upon it the vocation of an infinite cipher: in turn and according to the appeals of our imagination, the symbol of Paris, of modernity, of communication, of science or of the nineteenth century, rocket, stem, derrick, phallus, lightning rod or insect, confronting the great itineraries of our dreams, it is the inevitable sign; just as there is no Parisian glance which is not compelled to encounter it, there is no fantasy which fails, sooner or later, to acknowledge its form and to be nouished by it; pick up a pencil and let your hand, in other words your thoughts, wander, and it is often the Tower which will appear, reduced to that simple line whose sole mythic function is to join, as the poet says, *base and summit,* or again, *earth and heaven.*

This pure—virtually empty—sign—is ineluctible, *because it means everything.* In order to negate the Eiffel Tower (though the temptation to do so is rare, for this symbol offends nothing in us), you must, like Maupassant, get up on it and, so to speak, identify yourself with it. Like man himself, who is the only one not to know his own glance, the Tower is the only blind point of the total optical system of which it is the center and Paris the circumference. But in this movement which seems to limit it, the Tower acquires a new power: an object when we look at it, it becomes a lookout in its turn when we visit it, and now constitutes as an object, simultaneously extended and collected beneath it, that Paris which just now was looking at it. The Tower is an object which sees, a glance which is seen; it is a complete verb, both active and passive, in which no function, no *voice* (as we say in grammar, with a piquant ambiguity) is defective. This dialectic is not in the least banal, it makes the Tower a

4

singular monument; for the world ordinarily produces either purely functional organisms (camera or eye) intended to see things but which then afford nothing to sight, what *sees* being mythically linked to what remains *hidden* (this is the theme of the voyeur), or else spectacles which themselves are blind and are left in the pure passivity of the visible. The Tower (and this is one of its mythic powers) transgresses this separation, this habitual divorce of *seeing* and *being seen;* it achieves a sovereign circulation between the two functions; it is a complete object which has, if one may say so, both sexes of sight. This radiant position in the order of perception gives it a prodigious propensity to meaning: the Tower attracts meaning, the way a lightning rod attracts thunderbolts; for all lovers of signification, it plays a glamorous part, that of a pure signifier, i.e., of a form in which men unceasingly put *meaning* (which they extract at will from their knowledge, their dreams, their history), without this meaning thereby ever being finite and fixed: who can say what the Tower will be for humanity tomorrow? But there can be no doubt it will always be something, and something of humanity itself. Glance, object, symbol, such is the infinite circuit of functions which permits it always to be something other and something much more than the Eiffel Tower.

In order to satisfy this great oneiric function, which makes it into a kind of total monument, the Tower must escape reason. The first condition of this victorious flight is that the Tower be an utterly *useless* monument. The Tower's inutility has always been obscurely felt to be a scandal, i.e., a truth, one that is precious and inadmissible. Even before it was built, it was blamed for being useless, which, it was believed at the time, was sufficient to condemn it; it was not in the spirit of a period commonly dedicated to rationality and to the empiricism of great bourgeois enterprises to endure the notion of a useless object (unless it was declaratively an *objet d'art,* which was also unthinkable in relation to the Tower); hence Gustave Eiffel, in his own defense of his project in reply to the Artists' Petition, scrupulously lists all the future uses of the Tower: they are all, as we might expect of an engineer, scientific uses: aerodynamic measurements, studies of the resistance of substances, physiology of the climber, radio-electric research, problems of telecommunication, meteorological observations, etc. These uses are doubtless incontestable, but they seem quite ridiculous alongside the overwhelming myth of the Tower, of the human meaning which it has assumed throughout the world. This is because here the utilitarian excuses, however ennobled they may be by the myth of Science, are nothing in comparison to the great imaginary function which enables men to be strictly human. Yet, as always, the gratuitous meaning of the work is never avowed directly: it is rationalized under the rubric of *use:* Eiffel saw his Tower in the form of a serious object, rational, useful; men return it to him in the form of a great baroque dream which quite naturally touches on the borders of the irrational.

This double movement is a profound one: architecture is always dream and function, expression of a utopia and instrument of a convenience. Even before the Tower's birth, the nineteenth century (especially in America and in England) had often dreamed of structures whose height would be astonishing, for the century was given to technological feats, and the conquest of the sky once again preyed upon humanity. In 1881, shortly before the Tower, a French architect had elaborated the project of a sun tower; now this project, quite mad technologically, since it relied on masonry and not on steel, also put itself under the warrant of a thoroughly empirical utility; on the one hand, a bonfire placed on top of the structure was to illuminate the darkness of every nook and cranny in Paris by a system of mirrors (a system that was undoubtedly a complex one!), and on the other, the last story of this sun tower (about 1,000 feet, like the Eiffel Tower) was to be reserved for a kind of sunroom, in which invalids would benefit from an air "as pure as in the mountains." And yet, here as in the case of the Tower, the naïve utilitarianism of the enterprise is not separate from the oneiric, infinitely powerful function which, actually, inspires its creation: use never does anything but shelter meaning. Hence we might speak, among men, of a true Babel complex: Babel was supposed to *serve* to communicate with God, and yet Babel is a dream which touches much greater depths than that of the theological project; and just as this great ascensional dream, released from its utilitarian prop, is finally what remains in the countless Babels represented by the painters, as if the function of art were to reveal the profound uselessness of objects, just so the Tower, almost immediately disengaged from the scientific considerations which had authorized its birth (it matters very little here that the Tower should be in fact useful), has arisen from a great human dream in which movable and infinite meanings are mingled: it has reconquered the basic uselessness which makes it live in men's imagination. At first, it was sought—so paradoxical is the notion of an empty monument —to make it into a "temple of Science"; but this is only a metaphor; as a matter of fact, the Tower is *nothing*, it achieves a kind of zero degree of the monument; it participates in no rite, in no cult, not even in Art; you cannot visit the Tower as a museum: there is nothing to see *inside* the Tower. This empty monument nevertheless receives each year twice as many visitors as the Louvre and considerably more than the largest movie house in Paris.

Then why do we visit the Eiffel Tower? No doubt in order to participate in a dream of which it is (and this is its originality) much more the crystallizer than the true object. The Tower is not a usual spectacle; to enter the Tower, to scale it, to run around its courses, is, in a manner both more elementary and more profound, to accede to a *view* and to explore the interior of an object (though an openwork one), to transform the touristic rite into an adventure of sight and of the intelligence. It is this double function I should like to speak of briefly, before passing in conclusion to the major symbolic function of the Tower, which is its final meaning.

The Tower looks at Paris. To visit the Tower is to get oneself up onto the balcony in order to perceive, comprehend, and savor a certain essence of Paris. And here again, the Tower is an original monument. Habitually, belvederes are outlooks upon nature, whose elements—waters, valleys, forests—they assemble beneath them, so that the tourism of the "fine view" infallibly implies a naturist mythology. Whereas the Tower overlooks not nature but the city; and yet, by its very position of a visited outlook, the Tower makes the city into a kind of nature; it constitutes the swarming of men into a landscape, it adds to the frequently grim urban myth a romantic dimension, a harmony, a mitigation; by it, starting from it, the city joins up with the great natural themes which are offered to the curiosity of men: the ocean, the storm, the mountains, the snow, the rivers. To visit the Tower, then, is to enter into contact not with a historical Sacred, as is the case for the majority of monuments, but rather with a new nature, that of human space: the Tower is not a trace, a souvenir, in short a culture; but rather an immediate consumption of a humanity made natural by that glance which transforms it into space.

One might say that for this reason the Tower materializes an imagination which has had its first expression in literature (it is frequently the function of the great books to achieve in advance what technology will merely put into execution). The nineteenth century, fifty years before the Tower, produced indeed two works in which the (perhaps very old) fantasy of a panoramic vision received the guarantee of a major poetic writing *(écriture):* these are, on the one hand, the chapter of *Notre-Dame de Paris (The Hunchback of Notre Dame)* devoted to a bird's-eye view of Paris, and on the other, Michelet's *Tableau chronologique.* Now, what is admirable in these two great inclusive visions, one of Paris, the other of France, is that Hugo and Michelet clearly understood that to the marvelous mitigation of altitude the panoramic vision added an incomparable power of *intellection:* the bird's-eye view, which each visitor to the Tower can assume in an instant for his own, gives us the world to *read* and not only to perceive; this is why it corresponds to a new sensibility of vision; in the past, to travel (we may recall certain—admirable, moreover—promenades of Rousseau) was to be thrust into the midst of sensation, to perceive only a kind of tidal wave of things; the bird's-eye view, on the contrary, represented by our romantic writers as if they had anticipated both the construction of the Tower and the birth of aviation, permits us to transcend sensation and to see things *in their structure.* Hence it is the advent of a new perception, of an intellectualist mode, which these literatures and these architectures of vision mark out (born in the same century and probably from the same history): Paris and France become under Hugo's pen and Michelet's (and under the glance of the Tower) intelligible objects, yet without— and this is what is new—losing anything of their materiality; a new category appears, that of concrete abstraction; this, moreover, is the meaning which we can give today to the word *structure:* a corpus of intelligent forms.

Like Monsieur Jourdain confronted with prose, every visitor to the Tower makes structuralism without knowing it (which does not keep prose and structure from existing all the same); in Paris spread out beneath him, he spontaneously distinguishes separate—because known—points—and yet does not stop linking them, perceiving them within a great functional space; in short, he separates and groups; Paris offers itself to him as an object virtually *prepared,* exposed to the intelligence, but which he must himself construct by a final activity of the mind: nothing less passive than the *overall view* the Tower gives to Paris. This activity of the mind, conveyed by the tourist's modest glance, has a name: decipherment.

What, in fact, is a panorama? An image we attempt to decipher, in which we try to recognize known sites, to identify landmarks. Take some view of Paris taken from the Eiffel Tower; here you make out the hill sloping down from Chaillot, there the Bois de Boulogne; but where is the Arc de Triomphe? You don't see it, and this absence compels you to inspect the panorama once again, to look for this point which is missing in your structure; your knowledge (the knowledge you may have of Parisian topography) struggles with your perception, and in a sense, that is what intelligence is: to *reconstitute,* to make memory and sensation cooperate so as to produce in your mind a simulacrum of Paris, of which the elements are in front of you, real, ancestral, but nonetheless disoriented by the total space in which they are given to you, for this space was unknown to you. Hence we approach the complex, dialectical nature of all panoramic vision; on the one hand, it is a euphoric vision, for it can slide slowly, lightly the entire length of a continuous image of Paris, and initially no "accident" manages to interrupt this great layer of mineral and vegetal strata, perceived in the distance in the bliss of altitude; but, on the other hand, this very continuity engages the mind in a certain struggle, it seeks to be deciphered, we must find *signs* within it, a familiarity proceeding from history and from myth; this is why a panorama can never be consumed as a work of art, the aesthetic interest of a painting ceasing once we try to *recognize* in it particular points derived from our knowledge; to say that there is a beauty to Paris stretched out at the feet of the Tower is doubtless to acknowledge this euphoria of aerial vision which recognizes nothing other than a nicely connected space; but it is also to mask the quite intellectual effort of the eye before an object which requires to be divided up, identified, reattached to memory; for the bliss of sensation (nothing happier than a lofty outlook) does not suffice to elude the questioning nature of the mind before any image.

This generally intellectual character of the panoramic vision is further attested by the following phenomenon, which Hugo and Michelet had moreover made into the mainspring of their bird's-eye views: to perceive Paris from above is infallibly to imagine a history; from the top of the Tower, the mind finds itself dreaming of the mutation of the landscape which it has before its eyes; through the astonishment of space, it plunges into the mystery of time, lets itself be affected by a kind of spontaneous anamnesis: it is duration itself which becomes panoramic. Let us put ourselves back (no difficult task) at the level of an average knowledge, an ordinary question put to the panorama of Paris; four great moments immediately leap out to our vision, i.e., to our consciousness. The first is that of prehistory; Paris was then covered by a layer of water, out of which barely emerged a few solid points; set on the Tower's first floor, the visitor would have had his nose level with the waves and would have seen only some scattered islets, the Etoile, the Pantheon, a wooded island which was Montmartre and two blue stakes in the distance, the towers of Notre-Dame, then to his left, bordering this huge lake, the slopes of Mont Valérien; and conversely, the traveler who chooses to put himself today on the heights of this eminence, in foggy weather, would see emerging the two upper stories of the Tower from a liquid base; this prehistoric relation of the Tower and the water has been, so to speak, symbolically maintained down to our own days, for the Tower is partly built on a thin arm of the Seine filled in (up to the Rue de l'Université) and it still seems to rise from a gesture of the river whose bridges it guards. The second history which lies before the Tower's gaze is the

Middle Ages; Cocteau once said that the Tower was the Notre-Dame of the Left Bank; though the cathedral of Paris is not the highest of the city's monuments (the Invalides, the Pantheon, Sacré-Coeur are higher), it forms with the tower a pair, a symbolic couple, recognized, so to speak, by Tourist folklore, which readily reduces Paris to its Tower and its Cathedral: a symbol articulated on the opposition of the past (the Middle Ages always represent a dense time) and the present, of stone, old as the world, and metal, sign of modernity. The third moment that can be read from the Tower is that of a broad history, undifferentiated since it proceeds from the Monarchy to the Empire, from the Invalides to the Arc de Triomphe: this is strictly the History of France, as it is experienced by French schoolchildren, and of which many episodes, present in every schoolboy memory, touch Paris. Finally, the Tower surveys a fourth history of Paris, the one which is being made now; certain modern monuments (UNESCO, the Radio-Télévision building) are beginning to set signs of the future within its space; the Tower permits harmonizing these unaccommodated substances (glass, metal), these new forms, with the stones and domes of the past; Paris, in its duration, under the Tower's gaze, composes itself like an abstract canvas in which dark oblongs (derived from a very old past) are contiguous with the white rectangles of modern architecture.

Once these points of history and of space are established by the eye, from the top of the Tower, the imagination continues filling out the Parisian panorama, giving it its structure; but what then intervenes are certain human functions; like the devil Asmodeus, by rising above Paris, the visitor to the Tower has the illusion of raising the enormous lid which covers the private life of millions of human beings; the city then becomes an intimacy whose functions, i.e., whose connections he deciphers; on the great polar axis, perpendicular to the horizontal curve of the river, three zones stacked one

after the other, as though along a prone body, three functions
of human life: at the top, at the foot of Montmartre, pleasure;
at the center, around the Opéra, materiality, business, commerce; toward the bottom, at the foot of the Pantheon,
knowledge, study; then, to the right and left, enveloping this
vital axis like two protective muffs, two large zones of habita-
tion, one residential, the other blue-collar; still farther, two
wooded strips, Boulogne and Vincennes. It has been observed
that a kind of very old law incites cities to develop toward
the west, in the direction of the setting sun; it is on this side
that the wealth of the fine neighborhoods proceeds, the east
remaining the site of poverty; the Tower, by its very implan-
tation, seems to follow this movement discreetly; one might
say that it accompanies Paris in this westward shift, which
our capital does not escape, and that it even invites the city
toward its pole of development, to the south and to the west,
where the sun is warmer, thereby participating in that great
mythic function which makes every city into a living being:
neither brain nor organ, situated a little apart from its vital
zones, the Tower is merely the witness, the gaze which discreetly fixes, with its slender signal, the whole structure—
geographical, historical, and social—of Paris space. This
deciphering of Paris, performed by the Tower's gaze, is not
only an act of the mind, it is also an initiation. To climb the
Tower in order to contemplate Paris from it is the equivalent
of that first journey, by which the young man from the prov-
inces went up to Paris, in order to conquer the city. At the
age of twelve, young Eiffel himself took the diligence from
Dijon with his mother and discovered the "magic" of Paris.
The city, a kind of superlative capital, summons up that
movement of accession to a superior order of pleasures, of
values, of arts and luxuries; it is a kind of precious world of
which knowledge makes the man, marks an entrance into a
true life of passions and responsibilities; it is this myth—no
doubt a very old one—which the trip to the Tower still allows

13

us to suggest; for the tourist who climbs the Tower, however mild he may be, Paris laid out before his eyes by an individual and deliberate act of contemplation is still something of the Paris confronted, defied, possessed by Rastignac. Hence, of all the sites visited by the foreigner or the provincial, the Tower is the first obligatory monument; it is a Gateway, it marks the transition to a knowledge: one must sacrifice to the Tower by a rite of inclusion from which, precisely, the Parisian alone can excuse himself; the Tower is indeed the site which allows one to be incorporated into a race, and when it regards Paris, it is the very essence of the capital it gathers up and proffers to the foreigner who has paid to it his initiational tribute.

From Paris contemplated, we must now work our way back toward the Tower itself: the Tower which will live its life as an object (before being mobilized as a symbol). Ordinarily, for the tourist, every object is first of all an *inside*, for there is no visit without the exploration of an enclosed space: to visit a church, a museum, a palace is first of all to shut oneself up, to "make the rounds" of an interior, a little in the manner of an owner: every exploration is an appropriation; this tour of the *inside* corresponds, moreover, to the question raised by the *outside:* the monument is a riddle, to enter it is to solve, to possess it; here we recognize in the tourist visit that initiational function we have just invoked apropos of the trip to the Tower; the cohort of visitors which is enclosed by a monument and processionally follows its internal meanders before coming back outside is quite like the neophyte who, in order to accede to the initiate's status, is obliged to traverse a dark and unfamiliar route within the initatory edifice. In the religious protocol as in the tourist enterprise, being enclosed is therefore a function of the rite. Here, too, the Tower is a paradoxical object: one cannot be shut up within it since what defines the Tower is its longilineal form and its open structure: How can you be enclosed within emptiness, how can you visit a line? Yet incontestably the Tower is visited: we linger within it, before using it as an observatory. What is happening? What becomes of the great exploratory function of the *inside* when it is applied to this empty and depthless monument which might be said to consist entirely of an exterior substance?

In order to understand how the modern visitor adapts himself to the paradoxical monument which is offered to his imagination, we need merely observe what the Tower gives him, insofar as one sees in it an object and no longer a lookout. On this point, the Tower's provisions are of two kinds. The first is of a technical order; the Tower offers for consumption a certain number of performances, or, if one prefers, of paradoxes, and the visitor then becomes an engineer by proxy; these are, first of all, the four bases, and especially (for enormity does not astonish) the exaggeratedly oblique insertion of the metal pillars in the mineral mass; this obliquity is curious insofar as it gives birth to an upright form, whose very verticality absorbs its departure in slanting forms, and here there is a kind of agreeable challenge for the visitor; then come the elevators, quite surprising by their obliquity, for the ordinary imagination requires that what rises mechanically slide along a vertical axis; and for anyone who takes the stairs, there is the enlarged spectacle of all the details, plates, beams, bolts, which *make* the Tower, the surprise of seeing how this rectilinear form, which is consumed in every corner of Paris as a pure line, is composed of countless segments, interlinked, crossed, divergent: an operation of reducing an appearance (the straight line) to its contrary reality (a lacework of broken substances), a kind of demystification provided by simple enlargement of the level of perception, as in those photographs in which the curve of a face, by enlargement, appears to be formed of a thousand tiny squares variously illuminated. Thus the Tower-as-object furnishes its observer, provided he insinuates himself into it, a whole series of paradoxes, the delectable contraction of an appearance and of its contrary reality.

The Tower's second provision, as an object, is that, despite its technical singularity, it constitutes a familiar "little world"; from the ground level, a whole humble commerce accompanies its departure: vendors of postcards, souvenirs, knicknacks, balloons, toys, sunglasses, herald a commercial life which we rediscover thoroughly installed on the first platform. Now any commerce has a space-taming function; selling, buying, exchanging—it is by these simple gestures that men truly dominate the wildest sites, the most sacred constructions. The myth of the moneylenders driven out of the Temple is actually an ambiguous one, for such commerce testifies to a kind of affectionate familiarity with regard to a monument whose singularity no longer intimidates, and it is by a Christian sentiment (hence to a certain degree a special one) that the spiritual excludes the familiar; in Antiquity, a great religious festival as well as a theatrical representation, a veritable sacred ceremony, in no way prevented the revelation of the most everyday gestures, such as eating or drinking: all pleasures proceeded simultaneously, not by some heedless permissiveness but because the ceremonial was never savage and certainly offered no contradiction to the quotidian. The Tower is not a sacred monument, and no taboo can forbid a commonplace life to develop there, but there can be no question, nonetheless, of a trivial phenomenon here; the installation of a restaurant on the Tower, for instance (food being the object of the most symbolic of trades), is a phenomenon corresponding to a whole meaning of leisure; man always seems disposed—if no constraints appear to stand in his way—to seek out a kind of counterpoint in his pleasures: this is what is called comfort. The Eiffel Tower is a comfortable object, and moreover, it is in this that it is an object either very old (analogous, for instance, to the ancient Circus) or very modern (analogous to certain American institutions such as the drive-in movie, in which one can simultaneously enjoy the film, the car, the food, and the freshness of the night air). Further, by affording its visitor a whole polyphony of pleasures, from technological wonder to haute cuisine, including the panorama, the Tower ultimately reunites with the essential function of all major human sites: autarchy; the Tower can live on itself: one can dream there, eat there, observe there, understand there, marvel there, shop there; as on an ocean liner (another mythic object that sets children dreaming), one can feel oneself cut off from the world and yet the owner of a world.

The
Harcourt
Actor

I N FRANCE, YOU ARE NOT AN ACTOR IF YOU
have not been photographed by Harcourt Studios. The
Harcourt actor is a god; he never does anything: he is caught
in repose.

A euphemism, borrowed from the society pages, accounts
for this posture: the actor is imagined to be "in town." Which
means, of course, an ideal town, that city of the players where
nothing exists but festivities and love affairs, whereas on stage
everything is work, that generous and demanding "gift." And
this reversal must be surprising to the highest degree; we must
be stricken with confusion to discover, hanging in the theater
lobby, like a sphinx at the entrance to the sanctuary, the
Olympian image of an actor who has shed the skin of the
frantic, too-human monster and at last recovers his timeless
essence. Here the actor takes his revenge: obliged by his
sacerdotal function to mime on occasion old age, ugliness, in
any case the dispossession of himself, he now recovers an ideal
visage, detached from the improprieties of the profession.
Leaving the "stage" for "town," the Harcourt actor in no way
abandons "dreams" for "reality." Quite the contrary: on
stage, well-built, bony, fleshy, thick-skinned under the grease-
paint; in town, smooth, sleek, pumiced by the virtue, aerated
by the gentle light of Harcourt Studios. On stage, sometimes
old, at least emphasizing some age or other; in town, eternally
young, fixed forever at the pinnacle of beauty. On stage,
betrayed by the materiality of a muscle-bound voice as over-
developed as a dancer's calves; in town, ideally silent, i.e.,

19

mysterious, filled with the profound secrecy we attribute to any beauty which does not speak. On stage, lastly, necessarily engaged in trivial, heroic, in any case effective gestures; in town, reduced to a face purged of all movement.

Further, this pure countenance is rendered utterly useless —i.e., luxurious—by the aberrant angle from which it is shot, as if Harcourt's camera, privileged to seize this non-terrestrial beauty, had to take up its position in the most improbable zones of a rarefied space, and as if this countenance floating between the theater's crude earth and "town's" radiant sky could only be momentarily ravished from its intemporal nature, then devoutly abandoned to its solitary and regal course; sometimes maternally plunged earthward, sometimes ecstatically raised, the actor's face seems to unite with his celestial home in an ascension without haste and without muscles, quite contrary to the onlooking humanity which, belonging to a different zoological class and capable of movement only by the legs (and not by the face), must return to its apartment on foot. (What we need is a historical psychoanalysis of truncated iconographies. To walk is perhaps—mythologically—the most trivial, hence the most human gesture. Every dream, every ideal image, every social preferment first suppresses the legs, either by portrait or by automobile.)

Reduced to a face, shoulders, hair, the actresses thereby testify to the virtuous unreality of their sex—whereby they are manifestly angels in town, after having been mistresses, wives, bitches, and soubrettes on stage. As for the men, with the exception of the young leads, who admittedly belong more or less to the angelic species, since their face remains, like the women's, in a posture of evanescence—the men promote their virility by some urban attribute, a pipe, a dog, glasses, a mantelpiece to lean on, objects trivial but necessary to the expression of masculinity, an audacity permitted only to the males of the species, and by which the actor "in town"

manifests in the fashion of gods and kings on a spree that he
has no fear of being, sometimes, a man like anyone else,
furnished with certain pleasures (pipe), affections (dog),
weaknesses (glasses), and even an earthly domicile (mantelpiece).

The Harcourt iconography sublimates the actor's materiality and prolongs a "stage" necessarily trivial, since it functions, by an inert and consequently ideal "town." A paradoxical status, it is the stage which is here reality; the town is
myth, dream, wonderland. The actor, rid of the too-fleshly
envelope of the profession, rejoins his ritual essence as hero,
as human archetype, located at the limit of the physical
norms of other men. The face here is a novelistic object; its
impassivity, its divine dough suspend everyday truth and
bestow the confusion, the delight, and finally the security of
a higher truth. By a scruple of illusion quite proper to a
period and a social class too weak both for pure reason and
for the powerful myth, the intermissions audience, to be
bored and on display, declares that these unreal faces are
indeed those of "town" and thereby acquires the rationalist
good conscience of assuming a man behind the actor; but at
the very moment of despoiling the mime, Harcourt summons
up a god, and everything, in this bourgeois public, at once
blasé and living on lies, everything is satisfied.

As a consequence, the Harcourt photograph is an initiation rite for the young player, a guild diploma, his real professional *carte d'identité.* Has he actually taken his proper place
if he has not yet touched the Harcourt Holy Ampulla? This
rectangle which first reveals his ideal head, his intelligent,
sensitive, or witty expression, depending on the role he offers
to life, is the formal document by which the whole of society
agrees to separate him from its own physical laws and assures
him the perpetual revenue of a countenance which receives
as a gift, on the day of this baptism, all the powers usually
refused, at least simultaneously, to ordinary flesh: a change-

less splendor, a seduction pure of any wickedness, an intellectual power which does not necessarily accompany the actor's
art or beauty.

Which is why photographs by Thérèse Le Prat or Agnès
Varda, for example, are avant-garde: they always bequeath
the actor his fleshly face and enclose it frankly, with an
exemplary humility, in its social function, which is to "represent" and not to lie. For a myth as alienated as that of actors'
faces, this choice is extremely revolutionary: not to embellish
the lobby with the classic Harcourts, spruced up, smoothed
out, angelized or virilized (depending on the sex), is an audacity few theaters can afford.

Conjugations

WHAT A LOT OF MARRYING GOES ON IN OUR illustrated papers: grand marriages (Marshal Juin's son and the daughter of an Inspector of the Fisc, the daughter of the Duc de Castries and Baron de Vitrolles), marriages for love (Miss Europe '53 and her childhood sweetheart), projected star marriages (Marlon Brando and Josiane Mariani, Raf Vallone and Michèle Morgan). Naturally, all these marriages are not apprehended at the same moment, for their mythological virtue is not the same.

The grand marriage (whether aristocratic or bourgeois) corresponds to the ancestral and exotic function of the nuptial: it is both the potlatch between the two families and the spectacle of this potlatch in the eyes of the crowd which surrounds the consumption of goods. The crowd is necessary; hence the grand marriage is always "taken" in the public square in front of the church; it is here that the money is burned and the assembly blinded by it; into the flames are flung uniforms and full-dress suits, swords and cravats (of the Legion of Honor), the Army and the Government, all the big parts of the bourgeois theater, military attachés (moved), a captain of the Legion (blind), and the Parisian crowd (stirred). Power, law, mind, heart, all these values of Order are flung together into the nuptials, consumed in the potlatch, but thereby instituted more solidly than ever, handsomely prevaricating the natural wealth of any union. A "grand marriage," we must not forget, is a fruitful operation of accountancy, which consists in shifting to the credit of

23

nature the heavy debit of Order, of absorbing into the public euphoria of the Couple "the sad and savage history of men": order is fed on Love; mendacity, exploitation, cupidity, all the social diseases of the bourgeoisie are redeemed by the truth of the couple.

The wedding of Sylviane Carpentier, Miss Europe '53, to her childhood sweetheart, the electrician Michel Warembourg, allows us to develop a different image, that of the happy hearth. Thanks to her title, Sylviane might have had a brilliant career as a star, might have traveled, made films, earned a lot of money; docile and modest, she renounced such "ephemeral glory" and, faithful to her past, married an electrician from Palaiseau. The young newlyweds are shown in the post-nuptial phase of their union, establishing the habits of their happiness and the anonymity of a minor comfort: furnishing the two-rooms-and-kitchen, eating breakfast, going to the movies, marketing.

Here the operation obviously consists of putting all the natural glory of the couple at the service of the petit-bourgeois model: that this happiness, by definition paltry, can be nonetheless *chosen*—that is what refloats the millions of Frenchmen (and women) who participate in it by their condition. The petite bourgeoisie can be proud of the allegiance of Sylviane Carpentier, just as once upon a time the Church gained power and prestige because some aristocrat's daughter took the veil: Miss Europe's modest wedding, her touching entrance, after so much glory, into the two-rooms-and-kitchen of Palaiseau—that is M. de Rancé choosing the Trappist Monastery, or Louise de La Vallière choosing Carmel: great glory for La Trappe, for Carmel, and for Palaiseau.

Here love-stronger-than-glory sustains the morale of the social status quo: it is not sensible to leave one's condition, it is glorious to return to it. In exchange for which, the condition itself can develop its advantages, which are essentially those of retreat. Happiness, in this universe, is to play

at a kind of domestic enclosure: "psychological" question-
naires, gadgets, puttering, household appliances, schedules,
the whole of this utensile paradise of *Elle* or *l'Express* glo-
rifies the closing of the hearth, its slippered introversion,
everything which occupies and infantilizes it, excusing it
from a broader social responsibility: "two hearts, one
hearth." Yet the world exists, too. But love spiritualizes the
hearth, and the hearth masks the slum: we exorcise misery
by its ideal image, poverty.

A star's marriage (to another star) is almost never presented except in its future aspect. What it develops is the
virtually pure myth of the Couple (at least in the case of
Vallone/Morgan); for Brando, social elements still prevail, as
we shall see in a moment). Conjugality is therefore at the
limit of the superfluous, relegated without precautions to a
problematic future: Brando is *going to* marry Josiane Mariani
(but only once he has made twenty new films); Michèle Morgan and Raf Vallone will *perhaps* form a new couple in civil
life (but first Michèle will have to get a divorce). Here we are
faced with a possibility given as assured insofar as its importance is marginal, subject to that very general convention
which insists that publicly marriage is always the "natural"
finality of coupling. What counts, under the guarantee of an
hypothetical marriage, is to make acceptable the couple's
carnal reality.

    The (future) marriage of Marlon Brando is still weighted
with social complexes, for this is the wedding of the shep-
herdess and the seigneur. Josiane, though the daughter of a
"modest" Bandol fisherman, is accomplished, for she has
completed the first part of her degree and speaks English
fluently (theme of the "perfections" of the marriageable girl),
and has managed to touch the most mysterious man of the
cinema, a kind of compromise between Hippolyte and some
fierce and solitary sultan. Yet this ravishing of a humble
French girl by the Hollywood monster is total only in its

reflex movement: the hero taken captive by love seems to pour all his glamour back on the little French town, the beach, the market, the cafés and groceries of Bandol: in fact, it is Marlon who is fecundated by the petit-bourgeois archetype of all the female readers of the illustrated weeklies. "Marlon," says *Une Semaine du Monde*, "Marlon, accompanied by his (future) mother-in-law and his (future) wife, takes a peaceful stroll before dinner, like any French petit-bourgeois." Reality imposes upon the dream its décor and its status, our petite bourgeoisie manifestly enjoying a phase of mythic imperialism. To the first degree, Marlon's glamour is of a muscular, Venusian order; to the second degree, however, it is of a social order: Marlon is consecrated by Bandol much more than he consecrates it.

Martians

A T FIRST THE MYSTERY OF THE FLYING SAU-
cers was quite earthly: it was supposed that the object
came from the unknown Soviet, from that world as stripped
of clear intentions as another planet. And this form of the
myth already contained in germ its planetary development;
if the Soviet-propelled saucer so readily became a Martian
engine, it is because our Western mythology attributes to the
Communist world the very otherness of a planet: the
U.S.S.R. is an intermediary world between Earth and Mars.

Only, in this process, the marvelous has changed meaning;
we have shifted from the myth of combat to the myth of
judgment. Mars, as it happens, until further notice, is impartial: Mars lands to judge Earth, but before condemning, Mars
wants to observe, to understand. The great U.S.S.R./U.S.A.
standoff is henceforth perceived as a guilty state, since the
danger is out of proportion to any justification; whence the
mythic recourse to a celestial surveillance, powerful enough
to intimidate both sides. Analysts of the future will be able
to explain the figurative elements of this power, the oneiric
themes which compose it: the roundness of the device, the
smoothness of its metal, that superlative state of the world
suggested by a substance without seams; *a contrario,* we
understand better everything in our perceptive field which
participates in the theme of Evil: angles, irregular planes,
noise, discontinuity of surfaces. All of which has been mi-
nutely posited in the novels of anticipation whose Martian
psychosis merely resumes such descriptions quite literally.

27

More significant, Mars is implicitly endowed with a historical determinism copied from that of Earth. If the saucers are
the vehicles of Martian geographers here to observe Earth's
configuration, as one American scientist has ventured to remark, and as many doubtless believe, it is because the history
of Mars has ripened at the same rhythm as that of our world,
and produced geographers in the very century when we have
discovered geography and aerial photography. The only advance is that of the vehicle itself, Mars thus being merely an
imagined Earth, endowed with perfect wings, as in all dreams
of idealization. Probably if we were to land in our turn on the
Mars we have constructed, we should merely find Earth
itself, and between these two products of the same History
we could not determine which was our own. For if Mars has
reached our stage of geographical knowledge, Mars too must
have had its Strabo, its Michelet, its Vidal de la Blache and,
step by step, the same nations, the same wars, the same
scientists, and the same inhabitants as ourselves.

Logic obliges Mars to have had the same religions as well,
especially our own, the religion of Frenchmen. Martians,
according to *Le Progrès de Lyon,* have necessarily had a
Christ; consequently they have also had a pope (whereupon
the schism begins): otherwise they couldn't be civilized
enough to invent the interplanetary saucer. For, according to
this journal, religion and technological progress are equally
the precious consequences of civilization, one cannot proceed
without the other: *It is inconceivable,* we are told, *that beings
who have achieved such a level of civilization that they can
reach us by their own means should be "pagans." They must
be deists, acknowledging the existence of a god and having
their own religion.*

Thus this whole psychosis is based on the myth of the
Identical, i.e., of the Double. But here as always, the Double
is ahead, the Double is a Judge. The East/West confrontation
is already no longer the pure combat of Good and Evil, but

28

a kind of Manichaean strife, flung before the eyes of a third Onlooker; it postulates the existence of a Super-Nature from the sky, for it is in the sky that the Terror exists: the sky is henceforth without metaphor, the field where atomic death appears. The judge is born in the same site where the executioner threatens.

Further, this Judge—or rather this Onlooker—has been carefully reinvested with ordinary spirituality, as we have just seen, and differs very little, all in all, from a mere earthly projection. For one of the constant features of all petit-bourgeois mythology is this impotence to imagine the Other. Otherness is the concept most antipathetic to "common sense." Every myth tends fatally to a narrow and, worse still, to what we might call a class anthropomorphism. Mars is not only Earth, it is petit-bourgeois Earth, it is the little district of mentality cultivated (or expressed) by the popular illustrated press. No sooner has it taken form in the sky than Mars is thus *aligned* by the most powerful of appropriations, that of identity.

Paris
Not
Flooded

DESPITE THE DIFFICULTIES OR THE DISASTERS
it might have caused for thousands of Frenchmen, the
flood of January 1955 partook of Festivity far more than of
catastrophe.

First of all, it displaced certain objects, refreshed our perception of the world by introducing into it certain unaccustomed and yet explicable points: we saw cars reduced to their
roofs, streetlamps truncated till only their tops rose above the
surface like water lilies, houses cut up like children's blocks,
a cat treed for several days. All these everyday objects seemed
suddenly separated from their roots, deprived of the reasonable substance *par excellence,* the Earth. This break had the
merit of remaining strange, without being magically threatening: the sheet of water acted like a successful but familiar
trick, people had the pleasure of seeing shapes modified but
still "natural," their minds could remain fixed on the effect
without regressing in anguish toward the obscurity of causes.
The flood convulsed normal optics without invoking the fan-
tastic; objects were partially obliterated, not distorted: the
spectacle was singular but reasonable.

Any considerable rupture of the everyday introduces Festivity: now, the flood not only seized upon and displaced
certain objects, it overwhelmed the very coenesthesia of landscape, the ancestral organization of horizons: habitual lines
of the survey map, curtains of trees, rows of houses, roads,
the riverbed itself, and that angular stability which so carefully prepares the forms of property, all this was blurred, 31

spread from angle to plane: no more paths, no more banks, no more directions; a flat substance which goes nowhere and which thereby suspends man's process, detaches him from reason, from a utensility of sites.

Certainly the most disturbing phenomenon is the very disappearance of the river: the thing which is the cause of all this turmoil is no longer, the water has no course, the ribbon of the river, that elementary form of all geographic perception, of which children are so rightly fond, shifts from line to plane, the accidents of space no longer have any context, there is no longer any hierarchy among river, road, fields, slopes, empty lots; the panoramic view loses its major power, which is to organize space as a juxtaposition of functions. Hence it is at the very center of our optic reflexes that the flood disturbs us. But this disturbance is not *visually* threatening (I am speaking of the newspaper photographs, our only truly collective means of consumption, with regard to the flood): the appropriation of space is suspended, perception is flabbergasted, but the total sensation remains calm, motionless, and pliant; our gaze is swept into an endless dilution; the break in the ordinary visual function is not on the order of a tumult: it is a mutation of which we see only the fulfilled character, which distances its horror.

To this pacification of the view, engaged by the overflowing of calm rivers into a suspension of the functions and the *names* of terrestrial topography, there corresponds of course a whole euphoric myth of movement: looking at the photographs of a flood, each spectator feels himself conveyed by proxy. Whence the great success of scenes in which we see boats riding down the street: such scenes are numerous, newspapers and readers have shown their eagerness to enjoy them. This is because in them we see achieved in reality the great mythic and infantile dream of walking-on-water. After thousands of years of navigation, the boat still remains a surprising object: it produces desires, passions, dreams: children at play or workers fascinated by a passing steamer, all see in it the very instrument of deliverance, the always astonishing solution of a problem inexplicable to common sense: to walk on water. The flood revives the theme, gives it the everyday street for piquant context; we row to the grocer's, the village priest enters his church in a canoe, a family does its shopping by dinghy.

To this kind of wager is added the euphoria of reconstructing the village or neighborhood, giving it new roadways, using it somewhat in the manner of a theatrical site, varying the childhood myth of the cabin by difficult access to the house-as-refuge, protected by water itself, like a moated castle or a Venetian palace. Paradoxically, the flood has created a more accessible world, manipulable with the kind of pleasure the child takes in wielding his toys, exploring and enjoying them. The houses are no more than cubes, the rails isolated lines, the herds shifted masses, and it is the little boat, the superlative toy of the childhood universe, which has become the possessive mode of this arranged, outspread, and no longer rooted space.

If we turn from myths of sensation to myths of value, the flood keeps the same tenor of euphoria: here the press has easily developed a dynamics of solidarity, and reconstructed, quite spontaneously, the flood as a unifier of mankind. This results essentially from the *foreseeable* nature of the difficulties: there was, for instance, something warm and active in the way in which the papers determined in advance the day of maximum flooding; the virtually scientific schedule assigned to the outbreak of the disaster could unite men in a rational elaboration of the remedy: dikes, land fills, evacuations. We are dealing here with the same industrious euphoria which brings in a harvest or a laundry before the storm, raises a drawbridge in an adventure story; in a word, combats nature by the mere weapon of time.

Threatening Paris, the flood could even drape itself in

something of the myth of '48: the Parisians built "bar-
ricades," defended their city with cobblestones against the
enemy river. The seduction of this legendary mode of resistance is sustained by a whole imagery of the siege wall, the
glorious trench, the rampart of sand built by children on the
beach in their hasty struggles against the tide. It seemed
nobler than pumping out cellars, which the papers turned to
little or no effect, the concierges failing to understand the
point of checking the water's onset by pumping it back out
into the flooding river. Better to develop the image of armed
mobilization, cooperation of the troops, motor-driven life
rafts, rescue "of infants, the sick and the elderly," a Biblical
stabling of herds, indeed the whole fever of Noah filling the
Ark. For the Ark is a happy myth: in it humanity takes its
distance with regard to the elements, concentrates itself and
elaborates the necessary consciousness of its powers, making
disaster itself provide evidence that the world is manageable.

Bichon

and

the Blacks

*M*ATCH HAS PRINTED A STORY WHICH HAS A good deal to say about our petit-bourgeois myth of the Black: a young couple, both professors, have made an expedition into Cannibal country to do some painting; they have taken with them their months-old baby, Bichon. *Match* goes into ecstasy over the courage of all three.

First of all, nothing is more irritating than heroism without an object. A society is in a serious situation when it undertakes to develop gratuitously the *forms* of its virtues. If the dangers incurred by baby Bichon (torrents, wild animals, diseases, etc.) were real, it was literally stupid to impose them, on the mere pretext of doing some painting in Africa and satisfying the dubious ambition of getting on canvas "a debauch of sun and light"; it is even more reprehensible to disguise this stupidity as a piece of bravery, all quite decorative and moving. We see how courage functions here: a formal and empty action, the more unmotivated it is, the more respect it inspires; this is a boy-scout civilization, where the code of feelings and values is completely detached from concrete problems of solidarity or progress. What we have is the old myth of "character," i.e., of "training." Bichon's exploits are of the same sort as the more spectacular feats of mountain climbing or balloon ascension: demonstrations of an ethical order, which receive their final value only from the publicity they are given. In our culture, there frequently corresponds to the socialized forms of collective sport a superlative form of star sport: here physical effort does not institute man's

35

apprenticeship to his group, but instead an ethic of vanity, an exoticism of endurance, a minor mystique of risk, monstrously severed from any concern with sociability.

The trip Bichon's parents made into a region situated quite vaguely and significantly labeled the Country of the Red Negroes, a kind of fictional site whose actual characteristics are skillfully attenuated but whose legendary name already proposes a terrifying ambiguity between the color of their painted skins and the human blood they supposedly drink—the trip is presented in the vocabulary of conquest: one sets out unarmed, no doubt, but "armed with palette and brush," just as if it were a hunting safari or a military expedition, made under ungrateful material conditions (the heroes are always poor, our bureaucratic society does not favor noble departures), but rich in courage—and in its splendid (or grotesque) uselessness. Baby Bichon is assigned the Parsifal role, contrasting his blondness, innocence, curls, and smile to the infernal world of black and red skins, scarifications, and hideous masks. Naturally, it is the white gentleness which emerges victorious: Bichon subjugates the "man-eaters" and becomes their idol (the White Men are definitely cut out to become gods). Bichon is a good little Frenchman, he tames and conquers the savages without firing a shot: at the age of two, instead of being perambulated in the Bois de Boulogne, he is already working for his country, just like his daddy, who, without our quite knowing why, leads the life of a cameleer and tracks down "looters" in the bush.

We have already divined the image of the Black taking shape behind this tonic little tale: first of all, the Black is frightening, he is a cannibal; and if we find Bichon heroic, it is because he in fact risks being eaten. Without the implicit presence of this risk, the story would lose all its shock value, the reader would not be scared; hence occasions are multiplied in which the white baby is alone, abandoned, carefree, and exposed in a circle of potentially threatening Blacks (the only entirely reassuring image of the Black is that of the *boy,* the domesticated barbarian, coupled, moreover, with that other commonplace of all good African stories: the *thieving boy* who vanishes with his master's things). With each image we are meant to tremble over what might happen: this is never specified, the narrative is "objective," but it actually depends on the pathetic collusion of white flesh and black skin, of innocence and cruelty, of spirituality and magic; Beauty subjugates the Beast, Daniel is nuzzled by lions, and a civilization of the soul triumphs over the barbarism of instinct.

The profound cunning of Operation Bichon is to display the world of the Blacks through the eyes of a white child: here everything will look like a Punch-and-Judy show. Now, since this reduction exactly corresponds to the image "common sense" provides of these exotic arts and customs, we merely confirm *Match*'s reader in his childish vision, settled a little deeper in that impotence to imagine others which I have already pointed out apropos of petit-bourgeois myths. Ultimately the Black has no complete and autonomous life: he is a bizarre object, reduced to a parasitical function, that of diverting the white man by his vaguely threatening *baroque:* Africa is a more or less dangerous *guignol.*

And now, if we will contrast with this general imagery (*Match:* approximately a million readers) the ethnologists' efforts to demystify the Black phenomenon, the rigorous precautions they have long since taken when obliged to employ such ambiguous notions as "Primitives" or "Archaic Societies," the intellectual probity of such men as Mauss, Lévi-Strauss, or Leroi-Gourhan confronting the old racial terms in their various disguises, we will better understand one of our major servitudes: the oppressive divorce of knowledge and mythology. Science proceeds rapidly on its way, but the collective representations do not follow, they are centuries behind, kept stagnant in their errors by power, the press, and the values of order.

We are still living in a *pre-*Voltairean mentality, that is what must be said over and over. For in the age of Montesquieu or of Voltaire, if we were astonished by the Persians or the Hurons, at least it was in order to grant them the benefit of ingenuity. Today Voltaire would not write up Bichon's adventures the way *Match* has done: instead, he would imagine some cannibal (or Korean) Bichon contending with the napalmized *guignol* of the West.

A
Sympathetic
Worker

KAZAN'S FILM *ON THE WATERFRONT* IS A GOOD example of mystification. It is about—as everyone doubtless knows—a handsome longshoreman, lazy and somewhat brutish (Marlon Brando), whose consciousness is gradually raised by Love and the Church (in the form of a shock-priest, Spellman-style). Since this consciousness-raising coincides with the elimination of a fraudulent and abusive union and seems to commit the longshoremen to resisting some of their exploiters, it has been suggested that this is a courageous, indeed a "leftist" film intended to reveal the worker problem to the American public.

As a matter of fact, we are being given, once again, that truth-vaccine whose latest mechanism I have discussed with regard to other American films; we project the exploitive functions of management onto a small group of gangsters, and by this minor confessed evil, posited as a trivial and awkward pustule, we disregard the real evil, we avoid naming it, we exorcise it.

Yet it suffices to describe objectively the "roles" of Kazan's film to establish its power as a mystification: here the proletariat is constituted by a group of feeble creatures, bending under a yoke they see clearly without having the courage to throw it off; the (capitalist) State is identified with absolute Justice, and is the only possible recourse against crime and exploitation: if the worker can contact the State, its police and its investigative bodies, he is saved. As for the Church, under the appearances of a showy modernism, it is nothing

39

2001

more than a mediating power between the worker's constitutive poverty and the boss-State's paternal power. At the end, moreover, all this minor itch of justice and consciousness subsides quickly enough, resolved in the great stability of a beneficent order where the workers work, the bosses fold their arms, and the priests bless them all in their appropriate functions.

It is the end, moreover, which betrays the film, at the moment when many supposed that Kazan had skillfully insinuated his leftism: in the last sequence, we see Brando managing by a superhuman effort to present himself as a conscientious good worker before the boss who is waiting for him. Now this boss is obviously a caricature, and it was said: look how Kazan has managed to ridicule the capitalists.

Here or never is a case where we should apply the method of demystification Brecht proposes, and examine the consequences of our identification with the film's leading character. It is obvious that Brando is a positive hero for us; despite his defects, the public gives him its heart, according to that phenomenon of participation outside of which we are generally reluctant to consider any entertainment possible. When this hero, still greater for having rediscovered his conscience and his courage, wounded, weak and yet tenacious, heads for the boss who will give him work, our communion is limitless, we identify totally and uncritically with this new Christ, we participate unreservedly in his Calvary. Now Brando's painful assumption leads, as it turns out, to the passive acknowledgment of the eternal boss: what is orchestrated for us, despite all the caricatures, is the *restoration of order;* with Brando, with the longshoremen, with all of America's workers, we put ourselves, in a spasm of victory and relief, back in the hands of an employer whose flawed appearance, however exposed, makes no difference whatever: we have long since been caught, snared in a fatal communion with this longshoreman who learns the meaning of social justice only to bestow it, in the form of homage, to American capital.

As we see, it is the *participational* nature of this scene which objectively makes it an episode of mystification. Taught to love Brando from the beginning, we can no longer criticize him at any particular moment or even acknowledge his objective stupidity. Now, it is precisely against the danger of such mechanisms that Brecht proposed his method of alienation. Brecht would have asked Brando to *show* his naïveté, to make us understand that, despite all the sympathy we may have for his misfortunes, it is even more important to perceive their causes and their remedies. We can sum up Kazan's mistake by saying that what should have been judged was much less the capitalist than Brando himself. For there is much more to expect from the rebellion of victims than from the caricature of their masters.

Power
and
"Cool"

IN GANGSTER FILMS, WE HAVE NOW COLLECT-
ed a considerable vocabulary of "cool" gestures; slack-
jawed molls puffing their smoke rings into the faces of as-
saulting men; Olympian snaps of the fingers to give the clean,
economical signal for a burst of gunfire; the gang leader's wife
imperturbably knitting through the most horrifying situations . . . *Grisbi* had already institutionalized this vocabulary
of detachment by giving it the warrant of a recognizably
French ordinariness.

The gangster world is above all a world of *sang-froid*.
Phenomena which common philosophy still judges to be considerable, such as the death of a man, are reduced to a dia-
gram, presented under the volume of an infinitesimal gesture:
two fingers snapped, and at the other end of our field of vision
a man falls down in the same convention of movement. This
universe of litotes, always constructed as an icy mockery of
melodrama, is also, as we know, the last universe of fantasy.
The exiguity of the decisive gesture has a whole mythological
tradition, from the *numen* of the ancient gods, who with a
nod overturned men's fate, down to the tap of the fairy's
wand. The firearm had doubtless distanced death, but in a
manner so visibly rational that it has been necessary to refine
the gesture in order to manifest, once more, the presence of
fate; which is, precisely, the "cool" of our gangsters: the
residue of a tragic movement which manages to identify
gesture and action within the slenderest volume.

I shall insist further on the semantic precision of this

43

world, on the intellectual (and not only emotive) structure of the entertainment. The Colt's abrupt extraction from the jacket in an impeccable parabola in no way *signifies* death, for the usage has long since indicated that we are dealing with a simple threat, whose effect can be miraculously reversed: the revolver's emergence here has not a tragic but merely a cognitive value; it signifies the appearance of a new peripeteia, the gesture is argumentative, not strictly terrifying; it corresponds to a certain inflection of reasoning in a play by Marivaux: the situation is reversed, what had been an object of conquest is abruptly lost; the ballet of revolvers makes time more labile, inserting into the narrative's itinerary certain returns to zero, regressive leaps analogous to those of the Monopoly board. The Colt is language, its function is to maintain a pressure of life, to elude time's closure; it is *logos,* not *praxis.*

The gangster's "cool" gesture, on the contrary, has all the concerted power of a halt; without excitement, swift in the infallible search for its terminal point, it severs time and questions rhetoric. Any "cool" asserts that only silence is effective: knitting, smoking, raising a finger, these operations impose the notion that real life is in silence and that the action has the rights of life and death over time. Thus the spectator has the illusion of a positive world which is modified only under the pressure of actions, never under that of words; if the gangster speaks, it is in images, for him language is merely poetry, the word has no demiurgic function: to speak is his way of being idle and showing it. There is an essential universe which is that of well-oiled gestures, always halted at a specific and foreseen point, a kind of *summa* of pure effectiveness: and then, over and above, there are a few festoons of slang, which are like the useless (and therefore aristocratic) luxury of an economy in which the only exchange value is the gesture.

44

But this gesture, in order to signify that it is identical with action, must smooth out any emphasis, be filed down to the perceptive threshold of its existence; it must have no more than the density of a link between cause and effect; here "cool" is the surest sign of effectiveness; in it, each man regains the ideality of a world surrendered to a purely gestural vocabulary, a world which will no longer slow down under the fetters of language: gangsters and gods do not speak, they nod, and everything is fulfilled.

Depth
Advertised

TODAY, AS I HAVE INDICATED ELSEWHERE, the advertising of detergents plays essentially on a notion of depth: dirt is no longer stripped from the surface, but expelled from its most secret cells. All advertising of beauty products is similarly based on a kind of epic representation of the intimate. The little scientific prefaces, meant to introduce (and to advertise) the product, ordain that it cleans in depth, relieves in depth, feeds in depth, in short, at any price, infiltrates. Paradoxically, it is insofar as the skin is first of all a surface, but a living, hence a mortal surface, likely to dry out and to age, that it readily assumes its role as a tributary of deep roots, of what certain products call the *basic layer of renewal.* Moreover, medicine makes it possible to give beauty a deep space (dermis and epidermis) and to persuade women that they are the product of a kind of germinative circuit in which the beauty of efflorescences depends on the nutrition of roots.

Hence the notion of depth is a general one, present in every advertisement. As to the substances which infiltrate and convert *within* this depth, an utter blank; all we are told is that it is a matter of (vivifying, stimulating, nutritive) *principles* or (vital, revitalizing, regenerative) *essences,* a whole Molièresque vocabulary, updated perhaps by a touch of scientism *(bactericide agent R-51).* No, the real drama of all this little psychoanalysis of puffery is the conflict of two warring substances which subtly oppose the advance of the "essences"

47

and the "principles" toward the field of depth. These two substances are water and grease.

Both are morally ambiguous: water is beneficent, for everyone can see that old skin is dry and that young skins are cool, pure (*of a cool moistness,* says one product); the firm, the smooth, all the positive values of fleshly substance are spontaneously perceived as made taut by water, swelled like a sheet on the line, established in that ideal state of purity, cleanness, and coolness to which water is the general key. In advertising terms, hydration of the depths is therefore a necessary operation. And yet the infiltration of an opaque body appears anything but easy for water: we imagine that water is too volatile, too light, too impatient to reach quite reasonably these cryptal zones where beauty is elaborated. And then, water, in this physics of the flesh and in a free state, water scours, irritates, returns to air, becomes part of fire; water is beneficent only when it is imprisoned, contained.

Greasy substances have the inverse qualities and defects: they do not refresh; their softness is excessive, too durable, artificial; we cannot establish a beauty campaign on the pure idea of creams, whose very density is perceived as an unnatural state. Doubtless, grease (more poetically known as *oils,* as in the Bible or the Orient) contains a notion of nutrition, but it is safer to exalt it as a vehicular element, a euphoric lubricant, conducting water to the skin's depths. Water is posited as volatile, aerial, fugitive, ephemeral, precious; oil, on the contrary, holds fast, weighs down, slowly forces its way into surfaces, impregnates, slides along the "pores" (characters essential to beauty advertising). Every campaign of beauty products therefore prepares a miraculous conjunction of these enemy liquids, declared henceforth complementary; diplomatically respecting all the positive values of the mythology of substances, this conjunction manages to impose the happy assurance that grease is conveyed by water, and that there exist certain aqueous creams, certain softnesses without luster.

Most of the new creams are therefore nominally *liquid, fluid, ultra-penetrating,* etc.; the notion of grease, for so long consubstantial with the very idea of a beauty product, is masked or complicated, corrected by liquidity, and sometimes even vanishes, giving way to the fluid *lotion,* to the spiritual *tonic,* gloriously *astringent* if it is to combat the skin's waxiness, modestly *special* if, on the contrary, it is to nourish those voracious depths whose digestive phenomena are pitilessly exposed. This public opening of the human body's interiority is moreover a general feature of the advertising of toilet products. "Decay is expelled (from the teeth, the skin, the blood, the breath)": France is having a great yen for cleanliness.

A Few Words from Monsieur Poujade

WHAT THE PETITE BOURGEOISIE RESPECTS most in the world is immanence: every phenomenon which bears its own term within itself by a simple mechanism of return, i.e., to put it literally, every *paid* phenomenon, is agreeable to this class. Language is made to accredit, in its figures, in its very syntax, this morality of the retort. For example, Monsieur Poujade says to Monsieur Edgar Faure: "You take responsibility for the break, you will suffer its consequences," and the world's infinity is spirited away, everything is restored to a brief but complete and airtight order, the order of payment. Beyond the mere content of the sentence, there is in the very balance of the syntax the affirmation of a law according to which nothing is achieved without an equal consequence, in which every human action is rigorously countered, recouped, in short, a whole mathematics of the equation reassures the petit bourgeois, makes him a world to the measure of his dealings.

This rhetoric of retaliation has its own figures, which are all figures of equality. Not only must every offense be averted by a threat, but even every action must be forestalled. The pride of "not being taken" is none other than the ritual respect for a numerative order in which to foil is to annul. Hence the reduction of the world to a pure equality and the observance of quantitative relations between human actions are triumphant states. To pay back, to counter, to generate the event from its reciprocal, either by turning the argument or by foiling—all this closes the world upon itself and produces a certain happiness; so that it is only natural we should pride ourselves on this moral bookkeeping: the petit-bourgeois flourish consists in eluding qualitative values, in opposing processes of transformation by a statics of equalities (an eye for an eye, effect vs. cause, merchandise vs. money, penny for penny, etc.).

Monsieur Poujade is well aware that the capital enemy of this tautological system is the dialectic, which he more or less confuses, moreover, with sophistry: we defeat the dialectic only by an incessant return to calculation, to the computation of human behavior, to what Monsieur Poujade, in agreement with etymology, calls Reason ("Will the rue de Rivoli be stronger than Parliament? the dialectic more valid than Reason?"). Indeed, the dialectic risks opening this world we have so carefully closed over its equalities; insofar as the dialectic is a technique of transformation, it contradicts the numerative structure of ownership, it escapes the petit-bourgeois limits, and is therefore first anathematized, then declared a pure illusion: once again degrading an old romantic theme (which then was a bourgeois one), Monseiur Poujade dispenses with all the techniques of the intelligence, asserting petit-bourgeois "reason" against the sophisms and dreams of academics and intellectuals discredited by their mere position outside a computable reality. ("France is stricken with an overproduction of men with diplomas, polytechnicians, economists, philosophers, and other dreamers who have lost all contact with the real world.")

We know now what petit-bourgeois reality is: it is not even what is seen, it is what is counted; now this reality, the narrowest any society has been able to define, has its philosophy all the same: it is "good sense," the famous good sense of the "little people," Monsieur Poujade says. The petite bourgeoisie, at least Monsieur Poujade's petite bourgeoisie (the butcher stall, the corner grocery), possesses good sense in its own right, in the fashion of a splendid physical appendage, a special organ of perception: a curious organ, moreover, since in order to see clearly it must first blind itself, refuse to go beyond appearances, accept as ready money the propositions of "reality," and declare anything which risks substituting an explanation for a retort to be null and void. Its role is to posit simple equalities between what is seen and what is, and to assure a world without stages, without transition, and without progression. Good sense is the watchdog of petit-bourgeois equations: it blocks up any dialectical outlets, defines a homogeneous world in which we are at home, sheltered from the disturbances and the leaks of "dreams" (by which we are to understand an uncountable vision of things). Human behavior being pure talion, good sense is that selective reaction of the mind which reduces the ideal world to certain direct mechanisms of retort, of what the French call *riposte*.

Thus Monsieur Poujade's language shows, once more, that the whole petit-bourgeois mythology implies the refusal of alterity, the negation of the different, the euphoria of identity, and the exaltation of "kind." In general, this equational reduction of the world prepares an expansionist phase in which the "identity" of human phenomena quickly establishes a "nature" and thereupon a "universality." Monsieur Poujade is not yet at the point of defining *good sense* as the general philosophy of humanity; it is still, in his eyes, a class virtue, already given, it is true, as a universal reinvigorant. And this is precisely what is sinister in Poujadism: that it has laid claim from the start to a mythological truth and posited culture as a disease, which is the specific symptom of all fascisms.

Adamov

and

Language

A S WE HAVE JUST SEEN, OUR POUJADIST GOOD
sense consists in establishing a simple equivalence between what is seen and what is. When an appearance is
decidedly too peculiar, this same common sense still has a
means of reducing it without relinquishing the mechanism of
equalities. This means is symbolism. Each time that something seen appears unmotivated, good sense calls in the heavy
cavalry of the symbol, admitted to the petit-bourgeois heaven
insofar as, despite its abstract tendency, it unites the visible
and the invisible in the form of a quantitative equality (this
is worth that): calculation is saved, and the world still abides.

Adamov having written a play about pinball machines, an
unwonted object in our bourgeois theater, which, as for stage
properties, knows only the adulterous bed, our popular press
has hastily spirited away the unaccustomed by reducing it to
a symbol. As soon as *it meant something,* it was less dangerous. And the more the criticism of *Ping-Pong* was addressed
to a mass readership *(Match, France-Soir),* the more it has
insisted on the play's symbolic character: be reassured, it's
only a symbol, the pinball machine simply signifies "the complexity of the social system." This strange stage property is
exorcised since it means something, since it is worth something.

Now, the pinball machine in *Ping-Pong* symbolizes nothing at all; it does not express, it produces; it is a literal object,
whose function is to engender, by its very objectivity, certain
situations. But once again our criticism is misled, in its thirst

55

for depth: these situations are not psychological, they are essentially *language situations*. Here is a dramatic reality which we will have to admit, ultimately, alongside the old arsenal of plots, actions, characters, conflicts, and other elements of the classic theater. *Ping-Pong* is a masterfully mounted network of language situations.

What is a language situation? A configuration of words likely to engender what *at first glance* seem to be psychological relations, not so much false as frozen in the compromise of a previous language. And it is this paralysis which, finally, annihilates psychology. To parody the language of a class or of a character is still to possess a certain distance, to lay claim to a certain *authenticity* (that virtue beloved of psychology). But if this borrowed language is general, always situated just this side of caricature, and covering the entire surface of the play with a variable pressure but without any fissure through which some cry, some invented speech might emerge, then human relations, despite their apparent dynamism, are as though vitrified, ceaselessly deflected by a kind of verbal refraction, and the problem of their "authenticity" vanishes like a lovely (and false) dream.

Ping-Pong is altogether constituted by a block of this language under glass, analogous, if you like, to those frozen vegetables which permit the British to enjoy in their winter the acidities of the spring; this language, entirely woven out of tiny commonplaces, partial truisms, scarcely discernible stereotypes, hurled with all the force of hope—or of despair —like the particles of a Brownian movement—this language is not, to tell the truth, a canned language, as was, for example, the concierge's jargon reconstituted by Henri Monnier; it is rather a delayed-action language, fatally formed in the character's social life, and which thaws, real and yet a little too acid or virid, in a later situation where its slight glaciation, a touch of vulgar, *learned* emphasis, have incalculable effects. The characters of *Ping-Pong* are a little like Michelet's Robespierre: *they think everything they say!* A profound remark which underlines man's tragic plasticity with regard to his language, especially when—final and astounding aspect of the misunderstanding—that language is not even quite his.

This will perhaps account for *Ping-Pong's* apparent ambiguity: on the one hand, a mockery of language is obvious, and on the other, this mockery is continually creative, producing perfectly living beings, endowed with a density of time which can even conduct them through an entire existence to death. This means precisely that in Adamov the language situations altogether resist both symbol and caricature: it is life which is parasitical to language, that is what *Ping-Pong* declares.

Hence Adamov's pinball machine is not a key—it is not D'Annunzio's dead lark or the door of one of Maeterlinck's palaces; it is an object which generates language; like a catalytic element, it constantly affords the actors a fragment of speech, makes them exist in the proliferation of language. *Ping-Pong's* clichés, moreover, do not all have the same density of memory, the same relief; that depends on who says them: Sutter the faker who makes up fine speeches, displays certain caricatural acquisitions, parades a parodic language which produces laughter at once ("Words, they're all traps!"). The paralysis of Annette's language is slighter, and also more pathetic ("Someone else's turn, Mister Roger!").

Each character in *Ping-Pong* seems thereby doomed to his verbal rut, but each rut is dug differently, and these differences of pressure create precisely what in the theater we call situations, i.e., possibilities and choices. Insofar as *Ping-Pong's* language is altogether acquired, having come from the theater of life, i.e., from a life itself given as theater, *Ping-Pong* is theater to the second degree. It is the very contrary of naturalism, which always proposes to amplify the insignificant; here on the contrary the spectacular aspect of life, of language, *sets* on the stage (as we say that ice *sets*). This mode of congelation is the very mode of all mythic speech: like *Ping-Pong*'s language, the myth is itself a speech frozen by its own doubling. But since we are concerned with theater, the reference of this second language is different: the mythic language plunges into Society, into a general History; while the language Adamov has experimentally reconstituted can double only a first individual language, for all its banality.

In all our theatrical literature I see only one author of whom it can be said, to some extent, that he, too, has constructed his theater on a free proliferation of language situations: this is Marivaux. Conversely, the theater which is most opposed to this dramaturgy of language situations is, paradoxically, a verbal theater: Giraudoux, for instance, whose language is sincere, i.e., plunges into Giraudoux himself. Adamov's language has its roots in the air, and we all know that, in the theater, whatever is exterior flourishes.

Racine
Is
Racine

I HAVE ELSEWHERE DISCUSSED THE PETIT-bourgeois predilection for tautological reasoning (*business is business,* etc.). Here is a splendid example, one quite frequent in the order of the arts: "*Athalie* is a play by Racine," an artist from the Comédie-Française reminds us before presenting her new production.

First of all, we might notice here a little declaration of war (against the "grammarians, controversialists, annotators, priests, writers, and artist" who have commented on Racine). And it is true that tautology is always aggressive: it signifies a choleric break between the intelligence and its object, the arrogant threat of an order in which we are not to think. Our tautologists are like masters tugging sharply on their dog's leash; thought must not range too widely, the world is filled with suspect and futile alibis, we must play our common sense close to the chest, reduce our leash to the distance of a computable reality. And if someone were to set about thinking about Racine? A great danger: the tautologist furiously cuts down whatever is growing around him, for it might smother him.

Recognizable in our artist's declaration is the language of that familiar enemy we have often encountered here, which is anti-intellectualism. We know the old saw: too much intelligence is ruinous, philosophy is a useless jargon, you must leave room for feeling, intuition, innocence, simplicity, art

59

dies of too much intellectuality, intelligence is not an artist's
virtue, the powerful creators are empirical, the work of art
escapes all system—in short, cerebrality is sterile. We know
that the war against intelligence is always waged in the name
of *good sense,* and here we are essentially applying to Racine
that kind of Poujadist "understanding" I have already
spoken about. Just as the general economy of France is
merely a dream with regard to French fiscality, the only
reality revealed to Monsieur Poujade's good sense, so the
history of literature and of thought, and *a fortiori* history
itself, is merely an intellectual hallucination with regard to a
very simple Racine, a Racine as "concrete" as the internal
revenue service.

Our tautologists employ another weapon of anti-intellectualism as well: the recourse to innocence. Armed with a divine
simplicity, they claim a true apprehension of the true Racine;
we all know this old esoteric theme: the virgin, the child,
simple and pure beings, see more clearly. In Racine's case,
this invocation to "simplicity" has a double power as an alibi:
on the one hand, it opposes the vanities of intellectual exege-
sis, and on the other (moreover, the point is virtually uncon-
tested), it claims for Racine an aesthetic *askesis* (the famous
Racinian purity), which obliges all who approach him to
accept a *discipline* (tune: *art is born of constraint . . .*).

Lastly, our actress's tautology contains what we might call
the myth of critical rediscovery. Our essentialist critics spend
their time rediscovering the "truth" of past geniuses; literature for them is a huge warehouse of lost objects, through
which they go hunting . . . or fishing. What they rediscover
there, no one knows, and that is precisely the major advantage of the tautological method: not to have to say. Our
tautologists would be quite embarrassed, moreover, to advance further: Racine himself, Racine degree zero, doesn't
exist. There are only Racine-adjectives: Racine-Pure Poetry,
Racine-Lobster (Montherlant), Racine-Bible (that of Ma-

dame Véra Korène), Racine-Passion, Racine-Realist, etc. In short, Racine is always something besides Racine, and this is what renders the Racinian tautology so illusory. We understand at least what such vacuity in definition affords those who brandish it so proudly: a kind of minor ethical salvation, the satisfaction of having militated in favor of a truth of Racine, without having to assume the risks which any somewhat positive search for the truth inevitably involves: tautology dispenses us from having ideas, but at the same time prides itself on making this license into a stern morality; whence its success: laziness is promoted to the rank of rigor. Racine is Racine: admirable security of nothingness.

Billy Graham

at

the Vel' d'Hiv'

SO MANY MISSIONARIES HAVE REGALED US
with the religious practices of "Primitives" that it is entirely regrettable a Papuan witch doctor didn't happen to be
at the Vel' d'Hiv' to describe the ceremony presided over by
Dr. Graham under the name of an evangelizing campaign.
There is a splendid piece of anthropological raw material
here, which seems moreover to be inherited from certain
"savage" cults, for we recognize in it under an immediate
aspect the three great phases of every religious action: Expectation, Suggestion, Initiation.

Billy Graham makes us wait for him: hymns, invocations,
any number of futile little speeches entrusted to supernumer-
ary pastors or to American impresarios (jovial introduction
of the troupe: pianist Smith, from Toronto, soloist Beverly,
from Chicago, "an artist of the American radio, who sings
the Gospel so marvelously"), a good deal of boosting pre-
cedes Dr. Graham, who is constantly announced and who
never appears. Here he is at last, but only to lead our curiosity
further, for his first speech is not the right one: he is merely
preparing the advent of the *Message*. And other interludes
prolong our expectation, warm up the hall, establish in advance a prophetic importance of this Message, which, according to the best traditions of such spectacles, begins by
making itself desired in order to exist the more readily after-
ward.

We recognize in this first phase of the ceremony that great
sociological recourse of Expectation which Mauss has stud-

63

ied and of which Paris has already had a very up-to-date example in the hypnotism séances of Le Grand Robert. Here, too, the Mage's appearance was postponed as long as possible, and by repeated false starts the public was wrought up to that troubled curiosity which is quite ready to see in fact what it is being made to wait for. Here, from the first minute, Billy Graham is presented as a veritable prophet, into whom we beg the Spirit of God to consent to descend, on this very evening in particular: it is an Inspired Being who will speak, the public is invited to the spectacle of a possession: we are asked in advance to take Billy Graham's speeches quite literally for divine words.

If God is really speaking through Dr. Graham's mouth, it must be acknowledged that God is quite stupid: the Message stuns us by its platitude, its childishness. In any case, assuredly, God is no longer a Thomist, He shrinks from logic: the Message is constituted by an outburst of discontinuous affirmations, without any kind of link, each of which has no content that is not tautological *(God is God).* The merest Marist brother, the most academic pastor would figure as decadent intellectuals next to Dr. Graham. Some journalists, deceived by the Huguenot décor of the ceremony (hymns, prayer, sermon, benediction), lulled by the lenitive compunction proper to Protestant worship, have praised Dr. Graham and his team for their sense of proportion, their restraint: we were expecting an outré Americanism, girls, jazz, jovial and modernist metaphors (there were two or three of these, all the same). Billy Graham has doubtless purged his sessions of anything picturesque, and the French Protestants have been able to accommodate him. Still, Billy Graham's manner breaks with a whole tradition of the sermon, Catholic or Protestant, inherited from ancient culture, a tradition which is that of a requirement to persuade. Western Christianity has always submitted for its exposition to the general context of Aristotelian thought, has always consented to deal with reason, even when accrediting the irrationality of faith. Breaking with centuries of humanism (even if the forms may have been hollow and petrified, the concern for a subjective Other has rarely been absent from Christian didacticism), Dr. Graham brings us a method of magical transformation: he substitutes suggestion for persuasion: the pressure of the delivery, the systematic eviction of any rational content from the proposition, the incessant break of logical links, the verbal repetitions, the grandiloquent designation of the Bible held at arm's length like the universal can opener of a quack peddler, and above all the absence of warmth, the manifest contempt for others, all these operations belong to the classic material of the music-hall hypnotist: I repeat, there is no difference between Billy Graham and Le Grand Robert.

Billy Graham at the Vel' d'Hiv

And just as Le Grand Robert ended the "treatment" of his public by a particular selection, picking out and calling up to the stage beside him the elect of hypnosis, confiding to certain privileged individuals the responsibility of manifesting a spectacular trance state, so Billy Graham crowns his Message by a material segregation of the Awakened: the neophytes who this evening, at the Vel' d'Hiv', among the posters for Super Dissolution and Cognac Polignac, "received Christ" under the action of the magic Message, are led to a private hall, and even—if they are English-speaking—to a still more secret crypt: whatever it is that happens there, inscription on the conversion lists, new sermons, spiritual conferences with "counselors," or collections, this new episode is an ersatz form of Initiation.

All this concerns us quite directly: first of all, Billy Graham's "success" manifests the mental fragility of the French petite bourgeoisie, a class from which the public for these meetings, it appears, is chiefly recruited; the plasticity of this public to alogical and hypnotic forms of thought suggests that there exists in this social group what we might call a situation of risk: a portion of the French petite bourgeoisie

65

is no longer even protected by its famous "good sense," which is the aggressive form of its class consciousness. But this is not all: Billy Graham and his team have insisted heavily and repeatedly on the goal of this campaign: "to awaken" France ("We have seen God do great things in America; an awakening in Paris would have an enormous influence throughout the world." "We want something to happen in Paris which will have repercussions throughout the world"). From all appearances, the optic is the same as Eisenhower's in his declarations concerning French atheism. France has made herself known the world over by her rationalism, her indifference to faith, the irreligion of her intellectuals (a theme common to America and the Vatican; moreover, a theme vastly overrated): it is from this bad dream that she must be awakened. The "conversion" of Paris would obviously have the value of a worldwide example: Atheism defeated by Religion in its own lair.

Clearly we are dealing with a political theme: France's atheism interests America only because atheism is seen as the incipient phase of Communism. "To awaken" France from atheism is to awaken her from the Communist fascination. Billy Graham's campaign has been merely a McCarthyist episode.

The Dupriez Trial

THE TRIAL OF GÉRARD DUPRIEZ (WHO MUR-
dered his father and mother without known motive)
exposes the crude contradictions in which our Justice is imprisoned. This has to do with the fact that History advances
unequally: the idea of man has changed a great deal in the
last hundred and fifty years, new sciences of psychological
exploration have appeared, but this partial promotion of History has not yet produced any change in the system of penal
justifications, because Justice is a direct emanation of the
State, and because our State has not changed masters since
the promulgation of the penal code.

It happens that crime is always *constructed* by Justice
according to the norms of classical psychology: the phenomenon exists only as an element of a linear notionality, must be
useful, or else it loses its essence, cannot be recognized. To
be able to name Gérard Dupriez's action, we had to find an
origin for it; hence the entire trial was committed to the
search for a cause, however small; there was nothing left for
the defense, paradoxically, except to claim for this crime a
sort of absolute state, stripped of all qualifications—to make
it, precisely, a *crime without a name.*

The prosecution, for its part, had found a motive—subsequently belied by the testimony: Gérard Dupriez's parents
had apparently opposed his marriage, and it was for this
reason that he killed them. Here we have the example of what
Justice regards as criminal causality: the murderer's parents
happen to be in the way; he kills them in order to suppress

the obstacle. And even if he kills them out of anger, this anger does not cease being a rational state, since it directly serves a purpose (which signifies that, in the eyes of Justice, the psychological facts are not yet compensatory, pertaining to a psychoanalysis, but still utilitarian, pertaining to an economy).

Hence it suffices that the action be abstractly useful for the crime to receive a name. The prosecution admitted the parents' refusal to countenance Gérard Dupriez's marriage only as the motive of a quasi-demential state, anger; it does not matter that rationally (in terms of that same rationality which a moment before established the crime) the criminal cannot hope for any profit or benefit from his action (the marriage is more certainly destroyed by the murder of the parents than by their resistance, for Gérard Dupriez did nothing to conceal his crime): we are content here with an amputated causality; what matters is that Dupriez's anger be motivated in its origin, not in its effect; we impute to the criminal a mentality sufficiently logical to conceive the abstract utility of his crime, but not its real consequences. In other words, it suffices that madness have a *reasonable* origin for us to be able to call it a crime. I have already described, in the Dominici case, the quality of penal reason: it is of a "psychological" and thereby "literary" order.

As for the psychiatrists, they have not admitted that an inexplicable crime thereby ceases to be a crime, they have left the accused his entire responsibility, thereby seeming at first glance to oppose the traditional penal justifications: for them the absence of causality in no way prevents us from calling the murder a crime. Paradoxically, it is psychiatry which here defends the notion of an absolute self-control, and leaves the criminal his guilt, even beyond the limits of reason. Justice (the prosecution) establishes the crime on the cause and thus leaves room for the possibility of madness; whereas psychiatry, at least our official psychiatry, seems to want to postpone the definition of madness as long as possible; it grants no value to determinism and revives the old theological category of free will; in the Dupriez trial, it plays the role of the Church handing over to the secular arm (Justice) the accused it cannot include in any of its "categories"; it even creates for this purpose a privative, purely nominal category: perversion. Hence, confronting a Justice born in the bourgeois era, trained consequently to rationalize the world by reaction against divine or monarchic arbitrary action, and showing as an anachronistic vestige the progressive role it might have played, official Psychiatry revives the very old notion of a responsible perversion, whose condemnation must be indifferent to any effort of explanation. Far from seeking to enlarge its domain, legal psychiatry hands over to the executioner the madmen whom Justice, more rational though timorous, asks for nothing better than to abandon.

Such are some of the contradictions of the Dupriez trial: between Justice and the defense; between psychiatry and Justice; between the defense and psychiatry. Other contradictions exist at the very heart of each of these powers: Justice, as we have seen, irrationally dissociating the cause from the result, tends to excuse a crime in proportion to its monstrosity; legal psychiatry readily renounces its own and sends the murderer back to the executioner precisely when the psychological sciences are daily accounting for a greater share of man; and the defense itself hesitates between the claim of an *advanced psychiatry,* which would recuperate each criminal as a madman, and the hypothesis of a magical "force" which apparently seized upon Dupriez, as in witchcraft's finest hour (plea of Maître Maurice Garçon).

Shock-
Photos

IN HER BOOK ON BRECHT, GENEVIÈVE SERREAU
referred to a photograph from *Match* showing the execution of Guatemalan Communists; she noted accurately that this photograph is not terrible in itself, and that the horror comes from the fact that *we are looking at it* from inside our freedom; an exhibition of Shock-Photos at the Galerie d'Orsay, very few of which, precisely, manage to shock us, paradoxically confirms Geneviève Serreau's remark: it is not enough for the photographer to *signify* the horrible for us to experience it.

Most of the photographs exhibited to shock us have no effect at all, precisely because the photographer has too generously substituted himself for us in the formation of his subject: he has almost always *overconstructed* the horror he is proposing, adding to the *fact,* by contrasts or parallels, the intentional *language* of horror: one of them, for instance, places side by side a crowd of soldiers and a field of skulls; another shows us a young soldier looking at a skeleton; another catches a column of prisoners passing a flock of sheep. Now, none of these photographs, all too skillful, touches us. This is because, as we look at them, we are in each case dispossessed of our judgment: someone has shuddered for us, reflected for us, judged for us; the photographer has left us nothing—except a simple right of intellectual acquiescence: we are linked to these images only by a technical interest; overindicated by the artist himself, for us they have no history, we can no longer *invent* our own reception of this synthetic nourishment, already perfectly assimilated by its creator.

Other photographers have tried to surprise, having failed to shock us, but the mistake in principle is the same; they have attempted, for example, to catch, with great technical skill, the rarest moment of a movement, its extreme point, the leap of a soccer player, the levitation of objects in a haunted house . . . But here again the spectacle, though direct and not at all composed of contrasting elements, remains too constructed; capture of the unique moment appears gratuitous, too intentional, the product of an encumbering will to language, and these successful images have no effect on us; the interest we take in them does not exceed the interval of an instantaneous reading: it does not resound, does not disturb, our reception closes too soon over a pure sign; the perfect legibility of the scene, its *formulation* dispenses us from receiving the image in all its scandal; reduced to the state of pure language, the photograph does not disorganize us.

Painters have had to solve this same problem of the acme of movement, but they have had far greater success. Under the Empire, for example, having to reproduce certain instantaneous views (a horse rearing, Napoleon extending his arm on the battlefield, etc.), painters have left movement the amplified sign of the unstable, what we might call the *numen,* the solemn shudder of a pose nonetheless impossible to fix in time; it is this motionless overvaluation of the ineffable—which will later, in the cinema, be called *photogeny*—which is the very site where art begins. The slight scandal of those exaggeratedly rearing horses, of that Emperor frozen in an impossible gesture, that persistence of expression, which we might also call rhetorical, adds to the reading of the sign a kind of disturbing challenge, sweeping the reader of the image into an astonishment less intellectual than visual, precisely because it fastens him to the surfaces of the spectacle,

72

to his optical resistance, and not immediately to its signification.

Most of the shock-photos we have been shown are false,
just because they have chosen an intermediate state between
literal fact and overvalued fact: too intentional for photography and too exact for painting, they lack both the scandal of
the latter and the truth of art: the photographer has made
them into pure signs, without consenting to give these signs
at least the ambiguity, the delay of a density. Hence it is
logical that the only true shock-photos of the exhibition
(whose principle remains quite praiseworthy) should be the
news-agency photographs, where the fact, surprised, ex-
plodes in all its stubbornness, its literality, in the very obviousness of its obtuse nature. The executed Guatemalans, the
grief of Aduan Malki's fiancée, the murdered Syrian, the
policeman's raised truncheon—these images astonish because at first glance they seem alien, almost calm, inferior to
their legend: they are visually diminished, dispossessed of
that *numen* which the painters would not have failed to add
to them (and rightly, since they were making paintings).
Deprived both of its song and its explanation, the *naturalness*
of these images compels the spectator to a violent interroga-
tion, commits him to a judgment which he must elaborate
himself without being encumbered by the demiurgic presence
of the photographer. Here we are indeed concerned with that
critical catharsis Brecht demands, and no longer, as in the
case of painting, with an emotive purgation: thus perhaps we
can rediscover the two categories of the epic and the tragic.
The literal photograph introduces us to the scandal of horror,
not to horror itself.

Two Myths

of

the New Theater

IF WE ARE TO JUDGE BY A RECENT FESTIVAL OF
young companies, the new theater angrily inherits the
myths of the old (so that it is hard to tell what it is that
distinguishes the one from the other). We know, for example,
that in the bourgeois theater the actor, "devoured" by his
role, is supposed to seem fired by a veritable conflagration of
passion. He must seethe at any price, i.e., burn and at the
same time spill over; whence the moist forms of this combustion. In one new play (which won a prize), the two male
partners spread themselves in liquids of all kinds, tears,
sweat, and saliva. It was as if we were watching a dreadful
psychological labor, a monstrous torsion of the internal tis-
sues, as if passion were a huge wet sponge squeezed by the
playwright's implacable hand. The intention of this visceral
tempest is comprehensible enough: to make "psychology"
into a quantitative phenomenon, to compel laughter or suffering to assume simple metrical forms, so that passion, too,
becomes a merchandise like any other, an object of commerce, inserted in a numerical system of exchange: I give my
money to the theater, in return for which I demand a clearly
visible, almost computable passion; and if the actor gives full
measure, if he can make his body work before my eyes without cheating, if I cannot doubt the trouble he takes, then I
shall declare the actor to be excellent, I shall evidence my joy
at having invested my money in a talent worthy of it, return-
ing it to me a hundredfold in the form of real tears, real sweat.

Combustion's great advantage is of an economic order: my spectator's money has a verifiable yield at last.

Naturally, the actor's combustion decks itself out in spiritualized justifications: the actor gives himself over to the demon of the theater, he sacrifices himself, allows himself to be eaten up from inside by his role: his generosity, the gift of his body to Art, his physical labor are worthy of pity and admiration; this muscular labor is acknowledged, and when, exhausted, drained of all his humors, he appears in front of the curtain at the end, we applaud him like a champion weight lifter or hunger artist, and we secretly suggest he go and restore himself somewhere, renew his inner substance, replace all that water by which he has measured out the passion we have bought from him. No bourgeois public resists so obvious a "sacrifice," and I suppose that an actor who knows how to weep or sweat on stage is always certain to triumph: the obviousness of his labor makes it unnecessary to judge further.

Another unfortunate element in the heritage of the bourgeois theater is the myth of the "find." Veteran directors make their reputation out of it. Playing *La Locandiera,* one young troupe flies the furniture from the ceiling for each act. Of course this is unexpected, and everyone marvels at the invention: the trouble is, there is no reason for it, the device is evidently dictated by an imagination at bay, craving something new at any price; since by now we have exhausted all the artificial methods for setting the stage, since modernism and the avant-garde have saturated us with those scene changes in full view where some servant comes—supreme audacity—and sets down three chairs before our very eyes, the director now resorts to the last free space, the ceiling. The method is quite gratuitous, a matter of pure formalism, but nevertheless: in the bourgeois public's eyes, staging is never anything but a technique of such finds, and certain "animators" are very indulgent as to these requirements: for them it is enough to invent. Here again, our theater relies on the harsh law of exchange: it is necessary and sufficient that the director's provisions be visible and that each of us can verify the yield on his investment: whence an art which seeks the swiftest possible issue and chiefly manifests itself as a discontinuous—and therefore computable—series of formal successes.

Like the actor's combustion, the "find" has its disinterested justification: the effort is to give it the warrant of a "style": flying the furniture from the ceiling will be presented as an offhand operation, in harmony with that climate of lively irreverence traditionally ascribed to *commedia dell-'arte.* Of course style is almost always an alibi, meant to elude the profound motivations of the piece: to give a Goldoni comedy a purely "Italian" style (harlequinade, mime, bright colors, half masks, dance movements, and the rhetoric of nimbleness) is a cheap way of avoiding any social or historical content, thwarting the acute subversion of civic relationships—in a word, it is a mystification.

It would be hard to overstate the ravages of "style" on our bourgeois stages. Style excuses everything, absolves us from everything, notably any historical reflection; it imprisons the spectator in the servitude of a pure formalism, so that the revolutions of "style" are themselves no more than formal: the avant-garde director will be the one who dares substitute one style for another (without ever resuming contact with the play's real basis), converting, like Barrault's production of *The Oresteia,* our tragic academicism into a voodoo festival. But this comes down to the same thing, and it gets us no further to replace one style by another: Aeschylus the Bantu author is no less false than Aeschylus the bourgeois one. In the art of the theater, style is a technique of evasion.

The
Tour de France
As Epic

THERE IS AN ONOMASTICS OF THE TOUR DE France which in itself tells us that these races are a great epic. The racers' names seem for the most part to come from a very old ethnic period, from an age when the "race," indeed, was audible in a little group of exemplary phonemes *(Brankart le Franc, Bobet le Francien, Robic le Celte, Ruiz l'Ibère, Darrigade le Gascon)*. Then, too, these names keep recurring; they form certain fixed points in the great risk of the ordeal, whose task is to fasten an episodic, tumultuous duration to the stable essence of the great characters, as if man were, above all, a name which enables him to master events: Brankart, Geminiani, Lauredi, Antonin Rolland, these patronymics are read as algebraic signs of valor, loyalty, treachery, or stoicism. It is insofar as the racer's Name is both nutriment and ellipsis that it forms the chief figure of a veritable poetic language, making legible a world in which description is finally useless. This slow concretion of the racer's virtues in the audible substance of his name ends, moreover, by absorbing all adjectival language: at the outset of their glory, the racers are provided with some epithet indicative of their nature. Later on, this is futile. One says: *elegant Coletto* or *Van Dongen the Batavian;* for *Louison Bobet,* nothing more is said.

In reality, entrance into the epic order is made by the name's diminution: Bobet becomes Louison, Lauredi Nello, and Raphael Geminiani—a hero twice crowned because he is both *good* and *valorous*—is sometimes called Raph and sometimes Gem. These names are trivial enough, somewhat affectionate and somewhat servile; they account in one and the same syllable for a superhuman value and an utterly human intimacy, which the journalist approaches familiarly, a little the way the Latin poets approached the intimacy of Caesar or Maecenas. In the cyclist's diminutive there is that mixture of servility, admiration, and prerogative which posits the people as a voyeur of its gods.

Diminished, the Name becomes truly public; it permits placing the racer's intimacy on the heroes' proscenium. For the true epic site is not the combat but the tent, the public threshold where the warrior elaborates his intentions, from which he hurls his insults, his challenges, and his confidences. The Tour de France is thoroughly familiar with this glory of a false private life in which affront and accolade are the intensified forms of human relation: in the course of a hunting trip in Brittany, generous Bobet publicly offered to shake hands with Lauredi, who no less publicly refused to do so. These Homeric quarrels have as their counterpart the praises which the great racers address to each other over the crowd's head. Bobet says to Koblet: "I'm sorry for you," and this remark all by itself traces the epic universe in which the enemy exists only in proportion to the esteem in which he is held. This is because there subsist in the Tour de France many vestiges of enfeoffment, that status which joined man to man in a virtually carnal manner. They embrace a good deal in the Tour. Marcel Bido, technical director of the French team, embraces Gem following his victory, and Antonin Rolland presses a fervent kiss on the hollow cheek of this same Geminiani. Here the accolade is the expression of a magnificent euphoria experienced in the presence of the closure and perfection of the heroic world. On the contrary, we must avoid attaching to this fraternal happiness all the sentiments of gregarity which seethe among the members of *the same team;* these sentiments are much murkier. Indeed, the perfection of public relations is only possible among the great stars: as soon as the "domestics" come on stage, the epic declines to a novel.

The Tour's geography, too, is entirely subject to the epic necessity of ordeal. Elements and terrain are personified, for it is against them that man measures himself, and as in every epic it is important that the struggle should match equal measures: man is therefore naturalized, Nature humanized. The gradients are *wicked,* reduced to difficult or deadly percentages, and the relays—each of which has the unity of a chapter in a novel (we are given, in effect, an epic duration, an additive sequence of absolute crises and not the dialectical progression of a single conflict, as in tragic duration)—the relays are above all physical characters, successive enemies, individualized by that combination of morphology and morality which defines an epic Nature. The relay is *hairy, sticky, burnt out, bristling,* etc., all adjectives which belong to an existential order of qualification and seek to indicate that the racer is at grips not with some natural difficulty but with a veritable theme of existence, a substantial theme in which he engages, by a single impulse, his perception and his judgment.

In Nature the racer finds an animated milieu with which he sustains exchanges of nutrition and subjection. A certain maritime relay (Le Havre–Dieppe) will be "iodized," will afford energy and color; another (the North), consisting of paved roads, will constitute an opaque, rugged nourishment: it will be literally "hard to swallow"; still another (Briançon–Monaco), being schistose, prehistoric, will ensnare the racer. All posit a problem of assimilation, all are reduced by a strictly poetic movement to their profound substance, and confronting each of them the racer dimly seeks to define himself as a total man at grips with a Nature-as-substance, and no longer merely with a Nature-as-object. Hence it is the movements of approach to the substance which count: the racer is always represented in a state of immersion and not in a state of advance: he plunges, he crosses, he flies, he sticks, it is his link to the ground which defines him, often in a state of anguish or apocalypse (the *terrifying* descent above Monte Carlo).

The relay which undergoes the strongest personification is that of Mount Ventoux. The main passes, Alpine or Pyrenean, hard as they are, remain despite everything passages, they are perceived as objects to pass over; the pass is a hole, it accedes with difficulty to the person; but Ventoux has the plenitude of the mountain, a god of Evil, to which sacrifice must be made. A veritable Moloch, despot of the cyclists, it never forgives the weak and exacts an unjust tribute of sufferings. Physically, Ventoux is dreadful: bare, bald (stricken with a dry seborrhea, according to *l'Équipe*), it is the very spirit of the Dry; its absolute climate (it is much more an essence of climate than a geographical space) makes it into an accursed terrain, a test site for the hero, something like a higher hell in which the cyclist will define the truth of his salvation: he will vanquish the dragon either with the help of a god (Gaul, *Phoebus's friend*), or else by a pure Prometheanism, opposing this god of Evil by a still harsher demon (Bobet, *Satan of the bicycle*).

The Tour thus possesses a veritable Homeric geography. As in the *Odyssey,* the race is here both a periplus of ordeals and a total exploration of the earth's limits. Ulysses reached the ends of the Earth several times. The Tour, too, frequently grazes an inhuman world: on Mount Ventoux, we are told, the racers have already left the planet Earth, encountering here unknown stars. By its geography, the Tour is thus an encyclopedic survey of human space; and if we were to refer to some Viconian schema of History, the Tour would represent in it that ambiguous moment when man strongly personifies Nature in order to confront it more readily and to free himself more completely.

Of course, the racer's adherence to this anthropomorphic Nature can only be fulfilled by semi-real means. The Tour commonly practices an energetics of Spirits. The strength the racer possesses in order to confront Earth-as-Man may assume two aspects: *form,* a state more than an impulse, a privileged equilibrium between quality of muscles, acuity of intelligence, and force of character; and *jump,* a veritable electric influx which erratically possesses certain racers beloved of the gods and then causes them to accomplish superhuman feats. *Jump* implies a supernatural order in which man succeeds insofar as a god assists him: it is *jump* that Brankart's mother prays to the Virgin for in Chartres Cathedral, and Charlie Gaul, glamorous beneficiary of grace, is precisely a *jump* specialist; he receives his electricity from an intermittent commerce with the gods; sometimes the gods inhabit him and he works wonders; sometimes the gods abandon him, his *jump* is exhausted. Charlie can do nothing more of any use.

Jump has a hideous parody, which is called *doping:* to dope the racer is as criminal, as sacrilegious as trying to imitate God; it is stealing from God the privilege of the spark. God, moreover, knows how to take revenge on such occasions: as the wretched Malléjac knows, a provocative *doping* leads to the gates of madness (punishment of the theft of fire). Bobet, on the contrary, cool and rational, has no experience of *jump;* he is a strong spirit who does his work himself; a specialist in *form,* Bobet is an entirely human hero who owes nothing to supernature and derives his victories from purely earthly qualities, promoted thanks to the humanist sanction *par excellence:* the will. Gaul incarnates the Arbitrary, the Divine, the Marvelous, Election, complicity with the gods; Bobet incarnates the Just, the Human, Bobet denies the gods, Bobet illustrates an ethic of man-by-himself. Gaul is an archangel, Bobet is Promethean, a Sisyphus who refuses to dump his rock on those very gods who have doomed him to be, so magnificently, only a man.

The dynamics of the Tour itself are obviously presented as a battle, but its confrontation being of a special kind, this battle is dramatic only by its décor or its marches, not strictly speaking by its shocks. Doubtless, the Tour is comparable to a modern army, defined by the importance of its matériel and the number of its servants; it knows murderous episodes, national funks (France encircled by the *corridori* of Signor Binda, director of the Italian *Squadra*), and the hero confronts his ordeal in a Caesarian state, close to the divine calm familiar to Hugo's Napoleon ("Gem plunged, clear-eyed, into the dangerous descent above Monte Carlo"). Still, the very action of the conflict remains difficult to grasp and does not permit itself to be established in duration. As a matter of fact, the dynamics of the Tour knows only four movements: to lead, to follow, to escape, to collapse. *To lead* is the hardest action, but also the most useless; to lead is always to sacrifice oneself; it is pure heroism, destined to parade character much more than to assure results; in the Tour, panache does not pay directly, it is usually reduced by collective tactics. *To follow,* on the contrary, is always a little cowardly, a little treacherous, pertaining to an ambition unconcerned with honor: to follow to excess, with provocation, openly becomes a part of Evil (shame to the "wheel-suckers"). *To escape* is a poetic episode meant to illustrate a voluntary solitude, though one unlikely to be effective, for the racer is almost always caught up with, but glorious in proportion to the kind of useless honor which sustains it (solitary escapade of the Spaniard Alomar: withdrawal, hautiness, the hero's Castilianism *à la* Montherlant). *Collapse* prefigures abandon, it is always horrible and saddens the public like a disaster: on Mount Ventoux, certain collapses have assumed a "Hiroshimatic" character. These four movements are obviously dramatized, cast into the emphatic vocabulary of the *crisis;* often it is one of them, in the form of an image, which gives its name to the relay, as to the chapter of a novel (Title: *Kübler's Tumultuous Grind*). Language's role is enormous here, it is language which gives the event—ineffable because ceaselessly dissolved into duration—the epic promotion which allows it to be solidified.

The Tour possesses an ambiguous ethic: certain knightly imperatives contantly mingle with the brutal demands of the pure spirit of success. It is an ethic which cannot or will not choose between the commendation of devotion and the necessities of empiricism. A racer's *sacrifice* to his team's success, whether self-generated or imposed by an arbiter (the technical director), is always exalted, but always argued as well. Sacrifice is great, noble, testifies to a moral plenitude in the exercise of a team sport, of which it is the great justification; but it also contradicts another value necessary to the complete legend of the Tour: realism. *There is no place for sentiment in the Tour,* this is the law which enlivens the spectacle's interest. Here the knightly ethic is perceived as the risk of a possible submission to fate; the Tour resolutely rejects anything which might seem to affect in advance the naked, brutal risks of combat. *The die is not cast,* the Tour is a confrontation of characters, it requires a morality of the individual, of solitary combat for life: the journalists' problem and preoccupation is to contrive for the Tour an *uncertain future:* throughout the 1955 Tour, protests were made against the general belief that Bobet was certain to win. But the Tour is also a sport, it requires an ethic of the collectivity. It is this contradiction, in truth one never resolved, which obliges the legend constantly to discuss and to explain the sacrifice, to recall each time the generous ethic which sustains it. It is because sacrifice is perceived as a sentimental value that it must tirelessly be justified.

Here the technical director plays an essential role: he guar-

85

antees the link between end and means, conscience and prag-
matism; he is the dialectical element that unites in a single
laceration the reality of evil and its necessity: Marcel Bidot
is a specialist in these Cornelian situations which require the
sacrifice, in one and the same team, of one racer to another,
sometimes even, which is even more tragic, of one brother to
another (Jean to Louison Bobet). Indeed, Bidot exists only as
the real image of a necessity of an intellectual order, and
which, for this reason, in a universe by nature emotional,
requires independent personification. Labor is carefully divided: for each group of ten racers, there must be a pure
mind, whose role, moreover, is in no way privileged, for here
the intelligence is functional, its only task is to represent to
the public the strategic nature of the competition: Marcel
Bidot is therefore reduced to the person of a meticulous
analyst, his role is to *meditate*.

Sometimes a racer takes the cerebral burden upon himself:
this is precisely the case with Louison Bobet and what constitutes the entire originality of his "role." In general, the racers' strategic power is slight, rarely exceeding the art of a few
clumsy feints (Kübler faking in order to deceive his adversary). In Bobet's case, this monstrous lack of division among
the roles engenders an ambiguous popularity, much more
uncertain than that of a Coppi or of a Koblet: Bobet thinks
too much, he is a *winner*, not a *player*.

This meditation of the intelligence between the pure ethic
of sacrifice and the harsh law of success translates a compos-
ite mental order, at once utopian and realistic, consisting of
vestiges of a very old ethic, feudal or tragic, and of new
requirements proper to the world of total competition. It is
in this ambiguity that the essential signification of the Tour
consists: the masterly amalgam of the two alibis, idealist and
realist, permits the legend to mask perfectly, with a veil at
once honorable and exciting, the economic determinisms of
our great epic.

But whatever the ambiguity of the sacrifice, it ultimately reintegrates an order of clarity insofar as the legend ceaselessly returns it to a purely psychological disposition. What saves the Tour from the discomforts of freedom is that it is by definition *the world of characterial essences.* I have already indicated how these essences were posited by a sovereign nominalism which makes the racer's name the stable depository of an eternal value (Coletto, elegance; Geminiani, regularity; Lauredi, treachery, etc.). *The Tour is an uncertain conflict of certain essences;* nature, customs, literature, and the rules successively relate these essences with each other: like atoms, they graze each other, hook together, repel each other, and it is from this interplay that the epic is born. I supply below a characterial lexicon of the racers, at least of those who have acquired a reliable semantic value; we can count on this typology, it is stable, we are indeed dealing with essences. One might say that here, as in classical comedy, and singularly in *commedia dell'arte,* though according to an entirely different order of construction (comic duration remains that of a theater of conflict, whereas the Tour's duration is that of fictive narrative), the spectacle is generated by an astonishment of human relations: the essences collide according to every possible figure.

I believe that the Tour is the best example we have ever encountered of a total, hence an ambiguous myth; the Tour is at once a myth of expression and a myth of projection, realistic and utopian at the same time. The Tour expresses and liberates the French people through a unique fable in which the traditional impostures (psychology of essences, ethics of combat, magism of elements and forces, hierarchy of supermen and servants) mingle with forms of a positive interest, with the utopian image of a world which stubbornly seeks reconciliation by the spectacle of a total clarity of relations between man, men, and Nature. What is vitiated in the Tour is the basis, the economic motives, the ultimate profit

87

of the ordeal, generator of ideological alibis. This does not keep the Tour from being a fascinating national phenomenon insofar as the epic expresses that fragile moment of History in which man, however clumsy and deceived, nonetheless contemplates through his impure fables a perfect adequation between himself, the community, and the universe.

Racers' Lexicon (1955)

BOBET (Jean). Louison's double is also his negative; he is the great victim of the Tour. He owes to his elder the total sacrifice of his person, "as a brother." This racer, ceaselessly demoralized, suffers from a serious infirmity: he thinks. His quality as an established intellectual (he is an English teacher and wears enormous glasses) commits him to a destructive lucidity: he analyzes his suffering and loses by introspection the advantage of a musculature superior to his brother's. He is *complicated,* hence unlucky.

BOBET (Louison). Bobet is a Promethean hero; he has a magnificent fighter's temperament, an acute sense of organization, he is a calculator, he aims realistically at *winning.* His problem is a touch of cerebrality (though less than his brother, being only a college graduate); he has experienced anxiety and wounded pride: he is bilious. In 1955, he had to face a heavy solitude: lacking Koblet and Coppi, having to struggle with their ghosts, without declared rivals, powerful and solitary, everything was a threat to him, danger could appear from anywhere and everywhere ("I need the Küblers and the Coppis, it's too difficult being the only favorite"). *Bobetism* consecrates a very special type of racer, in whom energy is paired with an analytical and calculating interiority.

BRANKART. Symbolizes the rising younger generation. Has caused his elders some anxiety. Magnificent on the straight

stretches, of a powerful and offensive humor, inexhaustible.
COLETTO. The most elegant racer in the Tour.
COPPI. Perfect hero. On the bike, he has every virtue. Formidable ghost.
DARRIGADE. Repellent Cerberus, but useful. Zealous servant of the Tricolor's cause, and for this reason forgiven for being a wheel-sucker, an intractable jailer.
DE GROOT. Solitary rider, taciturn Batavian.
GAUL. New archangel of the mountain. Carefree ephebe, slender cherub, beardless boy, delicate and insolent, inspired youth, he is the Rimbaud of the Tour. At certain moments, Gaul is inhabited by a god; his supernatural gifts then hang a mysterious threat over his rivals. The divine gift given to Gaul is lightness: by grace, elevation, and soaring (the mysterious absence of effort), Gaul suggests a bird or a plane (he perches lightly on the spurs of the Alps, and his pedals turn like propellers). But sometimes, too, the god abandons him, his gaze then becomes "strangely blank." Like every mythic being that has the power of vanquishing air or water, Gaul, on earth, becomes clumsy, impotent; the divine gift encumbers him ("I can race only in the mountains. And even then, only uphill. Coming down, I'm clumsy, *or perhaps too light*").
GEMINIANI (called Raph or Gem). Races with the loyal and slightly obtuse regularity of a motor. Uninspired in the mountains. Out of favor and sympathetic. Talkative.
HASSENFORDER (called Hassen the Magnificent or Hassen the Corsair). A combative and conceited racer ("I've got a Bobet in each leg"). The ardent warrior who knows nothing but fighting, cannot fake.
KOBLET. Charmed racer who could permit himself anything, even not calculating his efforts. The anti-Bobet, for whom he remains, even absent, a formidable ghost, like Coppi.
KÜBLER (called Ferdi or the Eagle of the Adziwil). Angular, ungainly, dry and whimsical, Kübler participates in the theme of the galvanic. His *jump* is sometimes suspected of

artificiality (does he use drugs?). An actor (coughs and limps only when you're looking). As a German-speaking Swiss, Kübler has the right and the duty to talk baby talk, like Balzac's Teutons and the Countess de Ségur's foreigners ("Ferdi unlucky. Gem always behind Ferdi. Ferdi not get away").

LAUREDI. The traitor, the villain of the Tour this year. This situation permits him to be openly sadistic: he tried to make Bobet suffer by becoming a fierce leech behind him. Forced to give it up: was this a punishment? in any case a warning.

MOLINERIS. The man of the last kilometer.

ROLLAND (Antonin). Mild, stoical, sociable. A good racer in the clinch, regular in his performances. Bobet's confidant. Cornelian debate: must he be offered up? Typical sacrifice, since it is unfair and necessary.

Agony
Columns

JOURNALISM TODAY IS QUITE A TECHNOCRA-
cy, and our weekly press is the bench of a veritable magis-
tracy of Conscience and Council, as in the Jesuits' finest days.
The morality involved is a modern one, i.e., not emancipated
but guaranteed by science, and for which we require less the
advice of the universal sage than that of the specialist. Thus
each organ of the human body (for we must start with the
concrete) has its technician, both pope and supreme scholar:
the Colgate dentist for the mouth, the "Doctor, tell me"
physician for nosebleeds, the Lux chemist for the skin, a
Dominican father for the soul, and the agony columnist of
certain women's papers for the heart.

The Heart is a female organ. To deal with it requires
therefore a competence in the moral order as special as the
gynecologist's in the physiological. The adviser therefore occupies her position thanks to the sum of her knowledge in
moral cardiology; but a characterial gift is also required, a
gift which is, as we know, the glorious mark of the French
practitioner (contrasted, say, with her American colleagues):
this gift is the alliance of an extensive experience, implying
a respectable age, with an eternal youth of the Heart, which
here defines the right to knowledge, to science. The adviser
thus participates in a powerful type, that of the *rough dia-
mond,* endowed with healthy frankness (to the point of bully-
ing), a great vivacity in repartee, an enlightened but confident
wisdom, and whose knowledge, real and modestly hidden, is

always sublimated by the open sesame of contentious bourgeois morality: *good sense.*

To the degree that the Column allows us to know them,
the women who consult it are carefully stripped of any specific condition: just as under the surgeon's impartial scalpel
the patient's social origin is generously put between paren-
theses, so under the adviser's gaze the postulant is reduced
to a pure cardiac organ. Only her quality as a woman
defines her: social condition is treated here as a useless
parasitical reality, which might hamper the concern for a
pure feminine essence. Only men, an exterior race which
forms the Column's "subject," in the logistic sense of the
word (what is talked about), are entitled to be social (as
they must, since they *earn*); hence a specific heaven can be
established for them: in general, it will be that of the successful businessman.

The Column's humanity reproduces an essentially juridical typology: far from any romanticism or from any actual
investigation of what has been experienced, it follows as
closely as possible a stable order of essences, that of the Civil
Code. Women's world is divided up into three classes, of
distinct status: *puella* (virgin), *conjux,* and *mulier* (unmar-
ried woman, widow, adulteress, but in any case presently
alone and possessing a certain amount of experience). Confronting this distribution is external humanity, the one which
resists or threatens: first of all, the *parentes,* those who possess the *patria potestas:* then the *vir,* the husband or the male,
who also wields the sacred right to subjugate the woman.
Recognizably, for all its fictive apparatus, the world of the
Heart is not improvised: it always reproduces, for better or
worse, fixed juridical relationships. Even when it says *I* in its
most lacerating or naïve voice, the Column's humanity exists
a priori only as a small number of fixed, named elements,
those of the familial institution: the Column postulates the

Family just when it seems to be taking as its liberating task the exposure of its interminable disputes.

In this world of essences, that of woman herself is to be threatened, sometimes by the parents, more often by the man; in both cases, juridical marriage is salvation, the resolution of the crisis; whether the man be adulterous, or a seducer (moreover, an ambiguous threat), or reluctant, it is marriage as a social contract of appropriation which is the panacea. But the very fixity of the goal compels, in cases of delay or failure (and this is by definition the moment when the Column intervenes), certain unreal procedures of compensation: the Column's vaccines against the man's aggressions or negligences all aim at sublimating defeat, either by sanctifying it in the form of sacrifice (keeping silence, not thinking about it, being kind, hoping), or by claiming it *a posteriori* as a pure freedom (keeping one's head, working, flouting men, linking arms with women).

Thus, whatever the apparent contradictions, the Column's morality never postulates for Woman any condition but a parasitical one: only marriage, by naming her juridically, makes her exist. Once again we find the very structure of the gynaeceum, defined as a closed freedom under the exterior gaze of man. The Column establishes Woman more solidly than ever as a special zoological species, a colony of parasites with interior movements of its own but whose limited amplitude is always brought back to the fixity of the guardian element (the *vir*). This parasitism, maintained under trumpet calls of Female Independence, naturally involves a complete impotence with regard to any opening onto the real world: under cover of a competence whose limits are loyally paraded, the adviser always refuses to take sides about problems which appear to exceed the functions proper to the Feminine Heart; frankness comes to a halt, modestly enough, at the threshold of racism or religion; this is because such

93

frankness constitutes a vaccine with a very specific use; its role is to infuse a conformist morality of subjection: onto the adviser is projected all the emancipation potential of the feminine species: in her, women are free by proxy. The apparent freedom of the advice makes unnecessary any real freedom of conduct: morality seems to be loosened a little, only to tighten a little more securely the constitutive dogmas of society.

The "Batory" Cruise

SINCE THERE ARE NOW TO BE BOURGEOIS TRIPS in Soviet Russia, the French press has begun to elaborate certain myths of assimilation with regard to the Communist reality. Messieurs Sennep and Macaigne, of *Le Figaro,* having embarked on the *Batory,* have written for their paper the sketch of a new alibi, the impossibility of judging a country like Russia in a few days. Hasty conclusions are no good, Monsieur Macaigne declares gravely, ridiculing his traveling companions and their generalizing mania.

It is quite entertaining to see a paper which promulgates anti-Sovietism from year to year on the basis of gossip a thousand times more improbable than an authentic stay in the U.S.S.R., however short, suffering a fit of agnosticism and wrapping itself in the noble cloak of an insistence on scientific objectivity, at the very moment when its envoys can at last approach what they used to speak of so readily and so decisively from a distance. This is because, for the requirements of his cause, the journalist divides up his functions, like Maître Jacques his garments. To whom do you want to speak? To Monsieur Macaigne the professional journalist who informs and who judges, in a word who *knows,* or to Monsieur Macaigne the innocent tourist who out of pure probity wants to draw no conclusions from what he sees? This *tourist* is a wonderful alibi here: thanks to him, one can look without understanding, travel without taking any interest in political realities; the tourist belongs to a subhumanity by nature deprived of judgment and who ridiculously exceeds his condition when he claims to have any. And Monsieur Macaigne mocks those of his fellow travelers who seem to have had the absurd notion of adding to the sights of the street a few figures, a few general facts, the rudiments of a depth possible in the knowledge of an unknown country: the crime of *lèse-tourisme,* i.e., of *lèse-obscurantisme,* which, at *Le Figaro,* is not forgiven.

Hence for the general theme of the U.S.S.R. as a permanent object of criticism has been substituted the seasonal theme of the street, the only reality granted to the tourist. The street has suddenly become a neutral terrain, where one can observe without claiming to conclude. But we discover what observations are involved. For this honest reserve never prevents tourist Macaigne from pointing out in the immediate life before him several awkward accidents likely to recall Soviet Russia's barbarous vocation: the Russian locomotives emit a long moan quite unrelated to the whistle of ours; the station platforms are wooden; the hotels are badly run; there are Chinese characters on the trucks (theme of the yellow peril); finally, a fact which reveals a truly retarded civilization, there are no bistros in Russia—nothing but pear juice!

But above all, the myth of the street allows him to develop the major theme of all bourgeois political mystifications: the divorce between the people and the regime. Even if the Russian people is saved, it is as the reflection of French liberties. That an old woman should burst into tears, that a dock worker (*Le Figaro* is social) should offer flowers to the visitors from Paris, has less to do with an emotion of hospitality than with the expression of a political nostalgia: the French bourgeoisie *en voyage* is the symbol of French freedom, French happiness.

Hence it is only when it has been illumined by the sun of capitalist civilization that the Russian people can be recognized as spontaneous, affable, generous. Then there will be nothing but advantages in revealing its overflowing kindness:

which always signifies a deficiency of the Soviet regime, a plenitude of Western happiness: the "indescribable" gratitude the young Intourist guide expresses to the doctor (from Passy) who offers him nylons certainly indicates the economic backwardness of the Communist regime and the enviable prosperity of Western democracy. As always (and I have remarked on the phenomenon apropos of the *Guide Bleu*), we pretend to treat as comparable terms privileged luxury and popular standing; we ascribe to the credit of all of France the inimitable "chic" of our Parisian toilette, as if all Frenchwomen dressed themselves chez Dior or Balenciaga; and we photograph the young Soviet women dazed by French fashions as if we were dealing with a primitive tribe stopped cold by the fork or the phonograph. In a general way, the trip to the U.S.S.R. serves chiefly to establish the bourgeois honors of Western civilization: Parisian gowns, locomotives which whistle rather than moan, the bistros, pear juice abandoned, and above all, the French privilege *par excellence:* Paris, i.e., a combination of grand couturiers and Folies-Bergère: it is this inaccessible treasure which, apparently, stimulates the Russians' dreams, according to the *Batory* tourists.

In the face of which the regime can remain faithful to its caricature, that of an oppressive order which maintains everything in the uniformity of machines. The waiter in the sleeping car having asked Monsieur Macaigne to return the spoon with his glass of tea, Monsieur Macaigne deduces (always in a great gesture of political agnosticism) the existence of a gigantic paperwork bureaucracy whose sole concern is to keep up the exact inventory of teaspoons. A new pasture for national vanity, quite proud of the disorder of the French. The anarchy of customs and of superficial behavior is an excellent alibi for order: individualism is a bourgeois myth which allows us to vaccinate the order and tyranny of class with a harmless freedom: the *Batory* brought the flabbergasted Russians the spectacle of a glamorous freedom, that of chattering during museum visits and "making jokes" in the subway.

No question but that "individualism" is a luxury product for export only. In France, and applied to an object of a quite different importance, it has, at least for *Le Figaro,* another name. When four hundred Air Force veterans, called up for North African service, refused to serve one Sunday, *Le Figaro* no longer spoke of the sympathetic anarchy and enviable individualism of the French: no longer any question here of museum or subway, but rather of colonial investments and big money; whereupon "disorder" was no longer the phenomenon of a glorious Gallic virtue, but the artificial product of a few "agents"; it was no longer glamorous but *lamentable,* and the *monumental lack of discipline* of the French, formerly praised with so many waggish and self-satisfied winks, has become, on the road to Algeria, a shameful treason. *Le Figaro* knows its bourgeoisie: freedom out front, on display, but Order back home, a constitutive necessity.

The Man
in the Street
on Strike

THERE ARE STILL PEOPLE FOR WHOM A strike is a *scandal:* i.e., not only a mistake, a disorder, or a misdemeanor, but a moral crime, an intolerable action which in their eyes is an offense to Nature. *Inadmissible, scandalous, revolting* are the words used of a recent strike by certain readers of *Le Figaro.* This is a language which dates, in fact, from the Restoration and which expresses its profound mentality; that was the period when the bourgeoisie, only recently in power, operated a kind of crasis between Morality and Nature, giving the one the protection of the other: fearing they would have to naturalize morality, they moralized Nature, pretended to identify the political and the natural order, and ended by declaring immoral everything which contested the structural laws of the society they were determined to defend. To Charles X's prefects as to *Le Figaro*'s readers today, a strike seemed first of all a challenge to the prescriptions of moralized reason: to strike is "to defy the world," i.e., to infringe less a civic than a "natural legality," to attack the philosophic basis of bourgeois society, that mixture of morality and logic which is *good sense.*

For the scandal proceeds from an inconsistency: a strike is scandalous because it affects precisely those whom it does not concern. It is reason which suffers and rebels: direct, mechanical, one might say computable causality, which has already appeared to us as the basis of petit-bourgeois logic in Monsieur Poujade's speeches—this causality is disturbed: a strike's effect is incomprehensibly remote from its cause,

99

quite escapes it, and it is this which is intolerable, shocking. Contrary to what we might suppose about petit-bourgeois dreams, this class has a tyrannical, infinitely sensitive notion of causality: the basis of its morality is not magical at all, but rational. Only, it is a linear, narrow rationality based on a virtually numerical correspondence of causes and effects. What this rationality lacks is obviously the notion of complex functions, the imagination of a remote operation of determinisms, of a solidarity of events which the materialist tradition has systematized under the name of totality.

Such a restriction of effects requires a division of functions. We might readily imagine that "men" are united: therefore, we oppose not man to man, but the striker to the ordinary man. The ordinary man (also called *the man in the street,* whose conglomeration receives the innocent name of *population:* we have already seen all this in Monsieur Macaigne's vocabulary)—the ordinary man is an imaginary, even algebraic character thanks to whom it becomes possible to break up the contagious dispersion of effects and to retain a reduced causality about which we will be able to reason calmly and virtuously. By arguing a special status in the worker's general condition, bourgeois reason breaks the social circuit and demands for its own profit a solitude which it is the strike's very function to deny: the strike protests against what is expressly addressed to it. The man in the street and the taxpayer (that other alias) are literally *characters,* i.e., actors promoted according to the needs of the cause to surface roles; their mission is to preserve the essentialist separation of social cells, which we know was the first ideological principle of the bourgeois revolution.

So that in effect we rediscover here a constitutive feature of the reactionary mentality, which is to disperse the collectivity into individuals and the individual into essences. What the entire bourgeois theater does to psychological man, setting Old against Young, Cuckold against Lover, Priest against Man of the World, the readers of *Le Figaro* do to the social being: to set striker against taxpayer is to constitute the world into a theater, to derive from the total man a special actor, and to oppose these arbitrary actors to each other in the lie of a symbolic structure which pretends to believe that the part is merely a perfect reduction of the whole.

This constitutes part of a general technique of mystification which consists in formalizing the social disorder as much as possible. For example, the bourgeoisie is not concerned, it says, to know which side in a strike is right or wrong: having divided the effects the better to isolate the only one which concerns it, the bourgeoisie claims to have no interest in the cause: the strike is reduced to a solitary incident, to a phenomenon we avoid explaining the better to manifest its scandal. Similarly, the public services worker, the civil servant will be abstracted from the working mass, as if the entire salaried status of these workers was somehow drawn to, fixed at, and subsequently sublimated in the very surface of their functions. This prejudiced reduction of the social condition makes it possible to dodge reality without abandoning the euphoric illusion of a direct causality which begins just where it is convenient for the bourgeoisie that it should: as the citizen suddenly finds himself reduced to the pure concept of the man in the street, so young draft-age Frenchmen wake up one morning sublimated into a pure military essence which will be virtuously taken for the *natural* point of departure of universal logic: military status thus becomes the unconditional origin of a new causality, which it will henceforth be monstrous to question: to contest this status can therefore in no case be the effect of a general and previous causality (the citizen's political consciousness) but only the product of accidents posterior to the operation of the new causal series: from the bourgeois point of view, a soldier's refusal to serve can only be the result of agents or alcohol, as if there existed no other good reasons for this action: a belief whose stupidity is exceeded only by its bad faith, since it is obvious that the contestation of a status can find its root and nourishment only in a consciousness which takes its distance with regard to that status.

We are dealing here with a new outbreak of essentialism. Hence it is logical that, in the face of the lies of essence and of party, the strike should posit the being and the truth of a totality. The strike signifies that man is total, that all his functions are connected with each other, that the roles of man in the street, taxpayer, and soldier are much too fragile to oppose the contagion of facts, and that in society all are concerned by all. By protesting that a strike is a disturbance to those it does not concern, the bourgeoisie testifies to a cohesion of social functions which it is the very goal of the strike to manifest: the paradox is that the petit bourgeois invokes the *naturalness* of his isolation at the very moment when the strike overwhelms him with the obviousness of his subordination.

African
Grammar

THE OFFICIAL VOCABULARY OF AFRICAN AF-
fairs is, as we might suspect, purely axiomatic. Which is
to say that it has no value as communication, but only as
intimidation. It therefore constitutes a *writing,* i.e., a language
intended to bring about a coincidence between norms and
facts, and to give a cynical reality the guarantee of a noble
morality. In a general way, it is a language which functions
essentially as a code, i.e., the words have no relation to their
content, or else a contrary one. It is a writing which we might
call cosmetic, because it aims at covering the facts with a
sound of language, or if we prefer, with the sufficient sign of
language. I should like to indicate briefly the way in which a
lexicon and a grammar can be politically committed.

BANDE/BAND (of outlaws, rebels, or civil criminals). —
This is the very example of an axiomatic language. The dispar-
agement of the vocabulary here serves in a precise way to deny
the state of war, which permits annihilating the notion of an
interlocutor. "No arguments with outlaws." The moraliza-
tion of language thus permits referring the problem of peace to
an arbitrary change of vocabulary.

When the "band" is French, it is sublimated under the
name of *community.*

DÉCHIREMENT/LACERATION (cruel, painful). —This
term helps accredit the notion of History's irresponsibility.
The state of war is masked under the noble garment of trag-

edy, as if the conflict were essentially Evil, and not a (remedi-able) evil. Colonization evaporates, engulfed in the halo of an impotent lament, which *recognizes* the misfortune in order to establish it only the more successfully.

Phraseology: "The government of the Republic is resolved to make all possible efforts in order to bring to an end the cruel lacerations Morocco is suffering." (Letter from Monsieur Coty to Ben Arafa.)

". . . the Moroccan people, painfully divided against itself . . ." (Declaration by Ben Arafa.)

DÉSHONORER/DISHONOR. —We know that in ethnology, at least according to Lévi-Strauss's very suggestive hypothesis, *mana* is a kind of algebraic symbol, intended to represent "an indeterminate value of signification, in itself without meaning and therefore capable of receiving any meaning, whose unique function is to fill a gap between signifier and signified." *Honor* is quite specifically our *mana,* something like a blank place in which we arrange the entire collection of inadmissible meanings and which we make sacred in the manner of a taboo.

Phraseology: "It would be to dishonor the Moslem populations to let it be supposed that these men could be considered in France as their representatives. It would also be to dishonor France." (Communiqué of the Ministry of the Interior.)

DESTIN/DESTINY. —It is at the very moment when the colonized peoples are beginning to deny the fatality of their condition that the bourgeois vocabulary makes the greatest use of the word *Destiny.* Like honor, destiny is a *mana,* in which we modestly collect the most sinister determinisms of colonization.

Naturally, Destiny exists only in a linked form. It is not military conquest which has subjected Algeria to France, it is a conjunction performed by Providence which has united two destinies. The link is declared indissoluble in the very period when it is dissolving with an explosiveness which cannot be concealed.

Phraseology: "We intend, as for ourselves, to give the peoples whose destiny is linked to ours a true independence within voluntary association." (Monsieur Pinay to the UN.)

DIEU/GOD. —Sublimated form of the French government.

Phraseology: "When the Omnipotent designated us to wield supreme power . . ." (Declaration by Ben Arafa.)

". . . With the abnegation and the sovereign dignity of which you have always given the example . . . Your Majesty thus intends to obey the will of the Almighty." (Letter from Monsieur Coty to Ben Arafa, dismissed by the government.)

GUERRE/WAR. —The goal is to deny the thing. For this, two means are available: either to name it as little as possible (most frequent procedure); or else to give it the meaning of its contrary (more cunning procedure, which is at the basis of almost all the mystifications of bourgeois discourse). *War* is then used in the sense of *peace,* and *pacification* in the sense of *war.*

Phraseology: "War does not keep measures of pacification from being taken." (General de Monsabert.) By which we are to understand that (official) peace does not, fortunately, prevent (real) war.

MISSION/MISSION. —This is the third *mana* word. Into it we can put whatever is wanted: schools, electricity, Coca-Cola, police operations, raids, death sentences, concentration camps, freedom, civilization, and the "presence" of France.

Phraseology: "You know, however, that France has a mission in Africa which she alone can fulfill." (Monsieur Pinay to the UN.)

POLITIQUE/POLITICS. —Assigned a limited domain: on
the one hand, there is France; and on the other, politics.
North African affairs, when they concern France, are not
within the domain of politics. When things become serious,
abandon Politics for the Nation. For men of the Right, Politics is the Left: *they* are France.

Phraseology: "To seek to protect the French community
and the virtues of France is not to engage in politics." (General Tricon-Dunois.)

In a contrary sense and bracketed with the word *conscience
(politics of conscience),* the word *politics* becomes euphemistic; it then signifies: a practical sense of spiritual realities, the
nuance which permits a Christian to set out in good conscience to "pacify" Africa.

Phraseology: ". . . To refuse service *a priori* in an army
imminently to serve in Africa, in order to avoid such a situation (to contradict an inhuman order), this abstract Tolstoy-
ism cannot be identified with a politics of conscience, for it
is no politics at all." (Dominican editorial in *La Vie intellec-
tuelle.*)

POPULATION/POPULATION. —This is a favorite word
of the bourgeois vocabulary. It serves as an antidote to the
excessively brutal *classes,* which moreover is "without reality." *Population* is meant to depoliticize the plurality of
groups and minorities by pushing individuals back into a
neutral, passive collection which is entitled to the bourgeois
pantheon only on the level of a politically unconscious existence. The term is generally ennobled by its plural: *the Moslem populations,* which does not fail to suggest a difference
in maturity between the Metropolitan unity and the plural-
ism of the colonized, France *gathering* beneath her what is
by nature diverse and numerous.

When it is necessary to make a disparaging judgment (war
occasionally compels such severities), we readily fraction the

population into *elements*. Elements are generally fanatic or manipulated. (For only fanaticism or unconsciousness can impel anyone to try to abandon colonized status.)

Phraseology: "The elements of the population which have been able to join the rebels under circumstances . . ." (Communiqué from the Ministry of the Interior.)

SOCIAL/SOCIAL. —*Social* is always bracketed with *economic*. This duo uniformly functions as an alibi, i.e., it announces or justifies on each occasion certain repressive operations, to the point where we might say that it signifies them. The *social* is essentially schools (France's civilizing mission, education of overseas peoples, gradually led to maturity); the *economic* is *interests,* always *obvious* and *reciprocal,* which *indissolubly* link Africa and Metropolitan France. These "progressive" terms, once suitably drained, can function with impunity as magical units.

Phraseology: "Social and economic domain, social and economic installations."

The predominance of substantives in the whole vocabulary, of which we have just provided a few samples, derives obviously from the huge consumption of concepts necessary to the cover-up of reality. Though general and advanced to the last degree of decomposition, the exhaustion of this language does not attack verbs and substantives in the same way: it destroys the verb and inflates the noun. Here moral inflation bears on neither objects nor actions, but always on ideas, "notions," whose assemblage obeys less a communication purpose than the necessity of a petrified code. Codification of the official language and its substantivation thus go hand in hand, for the myth is fundamentally nominal, insofar as nomination is the first procedure of distraction.

The verb undergoes a curious legerdemain: if it is a main verb, we find it reduced to the state of a simple copula, meant simply to posit the existence or the quality of the myth. (Monsieur Pinay to the UN: *"There would be* an illusory détente . . . *it would be* inconceivable . . . *What would be* a nominal independence? . . ."* etc.) The verb arduously attains full semantic status only on the level of the future, the possible, or the unintentional, in a remote distance where the myth runs less risk of being contradicted. (A Moroccan government *will be constituted* . . . *called upon to negotiate* reforms . . . the effort undertaken by France *with a view to constructing* a free association . . . etc.)

In its presentation, the substantive generally requires what two excellent grammarians, Damourette and Pichon, who lacked neither rigor nor humor in their terminology, used to call: the *notorious plate,* which means that the substance of the noun is always presented to us as known. We are here at the very heart of the myth's formation: it is because France's *mission,* the *laceration* of the Moroccan people, or the *destiny* of Algeria are given grammatically as postulates (a quality generally conferred upon them by the use of the definite article) that we cannot contest them discursively. Notoriety is the first form of naturalization.

I have already observed the quite banal emphasis put on certain plural forms *(populations).* It must be added that this emphasis overvalues or depreciates at will certain intentions: *populations* installs a euphoric sentiment of pacifically subjugated multitudes; but when we speak of *elementary nationalisms,* the plural aims at degrading further, if it is possible, the notion of (enemy) nationalism, by reducing it to a collection of mediocre units. This is what our two grammarians, experts *avant la lettre* in African affairs, had further foreseen by distinguishing the *massive plural* from the *numerative plural:* in the first expression, the plural flatters an idea of mass; in the second, it insinuates an idea of division. Thus grammar inflects the myth: it delegates its plurals to different moral tasks.

The adjective (or the adverb) often plays a curiously ambiguous role: it seems to proceed from an anxiety, from the sentiment that the substantives used, despite their notorious character, have undergone a wear and tear which cannot be entirely concealed; whence the necessity to reinvigorate them: independence becomes *true,* aspirations *authentic,* destinies *indissolubly* linked. Here the adjective aims at clearing the noun of its past disappointments, presenting it in a new, innocent, credible state. As in the case of main verbs, the adjective confers a future value upon discourse. Past and present are the business of the substantives, great concepts in which the idea alone dispenses us from proof (Mission, Independence, Friendship, Cooperation, etc.); action and predicate, in order to be irrefutable, must take shelter behind some unreal form: finality, promise, or adjuration.

Unfortunately, these adjectives of reinvigoration are worn out almost as fast as they are used, so that it is finally the adjectival relaunching of the myth which most certainly designates its inflation. It suffices to read *true, authentic, indissoluble,* or *unanimous* to get wind of the emptiness of the rhetoric. This is because at bottom these adjectives, which we might call adjectives of essence, because they develop under a modal form the substance of the name they accompany—these adjectives cannot modify anything: independence cannot be anything but independent, friendship friendly, and cooperation unanimous. By the impotence of their effort, these wretched adjectives here come to manifest the ultimate health of language. Try as the official rhetoric will to reinforce the coverings of reality, there is a moment when the words resist it and oblige it to reveal beneath the myth the alternative of lie or truth: independence is or is not, and all the adjectival designs which strive to give nothingness the qualities of being are the very signature of culpability.

Literature
according to
Minou Drouet

THE MINOU DROUET AFFAIR HAS FOR SOME time come to look like a detective story: did she do it, or didn't she? To this mystery have been applied the habitual police methods (minus torture, and even then!): questioning, sequestration, graphology, psychotechniques, and internal analysis of the documents. If society has mobilized a quasi-judiciary machinery in order to solve a "poetic" riddle, we suspect it has not done so out of a simple love of poetry; it is because the image of a child-poet is both surprising and necessary: this is an image which must be authenticated in as scientific a manner as possible insofar as it governs the central myth of bourgeois art: the myth of irresponsibility (of which the genius, the child, and the poet are merely the sublimated figures).

Until the discovery of objective documents, all those who have taken part in the police investigation (and they are numerous, indeed) have had to rely solely on a certain normative idea of childhood and of poetry, the idea which they have in themselves. The arguments made about the Minou Drouet case are by nature tautological, they have no demonstrative value: I cannot prove that the verses shown to me are really a child's if I do not first know what childhood is and what poetry is: which comes down to closing the trial over itself. This is a new example of that illusory detective science which functioned so furiously in the case of old Dominici: completely based on a certain tyranny of *likelihood,* it constructs a circular truth which carefully leaves out the reality of the accused or of the problem: every police inquiry of this kind consists in uniting the postulates we ourselves have posited from the beginning: to be guilty, for old Dominici, was to coincide with the "psychology" which the chief prosecutor carries within himself; it was to assume, in the fashion of a magical transference, the guilty man who is inside the magistrates; it was to constitute oneself as a scapegoat, the *likelihood* never being anything but the accused's disposition to resemble his judges. Similarly, to question oneself (furiously, as has been done in the press) as to the authenticity of Drouetist poetry is to start with a prejudice as to childhood and as to poetry, and whatever we find on the way, to return to it inevitably; it is to postulate both a poetic and a childhood normality, by virtue of which we will judge Minou Drouet; it is, whatever we decide, to enjoin Minou Drouet to take the burden upon herself, at once as prodigy and as victim, as mystery and as product, i.e., ultimately as pure magical object, with the entire poetic myth and the entire childhood myth of our time.

Moreover, it is the variable combination of these two myths which produces the difference in our reactions and our judgments. Three mythological ages are represented here: a few belated classics, hostile by tradition to poetry-as-disorder, condemn Minou Drouet in any case: if her poetry is authentic, it is the poetry of a child, hence it is suspect, not being "reasonable"; and if it is the poetry of an adult, they condemn it because then it is false. Closer to our own time, proud to accede to an irrational poetry, a group of venerable neophytes are agog at having discovered (in 1955) the poetic power of childhood, calling "a miracle" a banal literary phenomenon, long since familiar; others, finally, the old militants of childhood-poetry, those who were at the myth's root tip when it was avant-garde, look skeptically askance at the poetry of Minou Drouet, wearied by the heavy memory of a heroic campagne, of a knowledge which nothing can any longer intimidate (Cocteau: "All children nine years old have genius, except Minou Drouet"). The fourth age, that of today's poets, seems not to have been consulted: virtually unknown to the public at large, it has been decided that their judgment would have no demonstrative value, insofar as they represent no myth: I doubt, moreover, that they recognize anything of themselves in the poetry of Minou Drouet.

But whether Minou's poetry is declared innocent or adult (i.e., whether it is praised or suspected) is in either case to acknowledge it to be based on a profound alterity posited by nature itself between childhood and maturity, it is to postulate the child as an asocial being, or at the very least as one capable of spontaneously applying its own criticism to itself and of forbidding itself the use of accepted words, with the sole purpose of manifesting itself fully as an ideal child: to believe in the poetic "genius" of childhood is to believe in a kind of literary parthenogenesis, to posit literature once again as a gift of the gods. Here all trace of "culture" is attributed to lying, as if the use of vocabularies were strictly governed by nature, as if the child did not live in a constant osmosis with the adult milieu; and metaphor, image, figures of speech are attributed to childhood as signs of pure spontaneity, whereas, consciously or not, they are the seat of a powerful elaboration, they suppose a "depth" in which individual maturity has a decisive part.

Whatever the results of the inquiry, the riddle is therefore of little interest, it enlightens us neither as to childhood nor as to poetry. What conclusively renders this mystery indifferent to us is that, whether childish or adult, this poetry has a perfectly historical reality: we can date it, and the least we can say is that it is a little older than eight, which is Minou Drouet's age. There were, as a matter of fact, around 1914, a certain number of minor poets whom the histories of our literature, deeply embarrassed to classify nothingness, generally group under the chaste name of Isolated and Belated,

Whimsical and Intimist, etc. It is incontestably here that we must put young Drouet—or her muse—alongside poets as glamorous as Mme Burnat-Provins, Roger Allard, or Tristan Klingsor. Minou Drouet's poetry is of their powers; it is a docile, sugary poetry, entirely based on the belief that poetry is a matter of metaphor, and whose content is nothing more than a kind of elegiac, bourgeois sentiment. That this homely preciosity can pass for poetry, and that the very name, in this regard, of Rimbaud, the inevitable child-poet, should be advanced is a pure derivation of the myth. Moreover, a very clear myth, for the function of these poets is obvious: they furnish the public the *signs* of poetry, not poetry itself; they are economic and reassuring. One woman has nicely expressed this superficially emancipated and profoundly prudent function of intimist "sensibility": Madame de Noailles, who (coincidentally!) prefaced the poems of another child "of genius," one Sabine Sicaud, dead at fourteen.

Authentic or not, this poetry is therefore dated—markedly so. But warranted today by a press campaign and the faith of several personalities, it gives us precisely what society believes to be childhood *and* poetry. Quoted, vaunted, opposed, the texts of the Drouet family are precious mythological raw material.

First of all, there is the myth of the genius, which we are certainly never done with. The classics had decreed that this was all a matter of patience. Today, genius is a way of gaining time, of doing at eight what we normally do at twenty-five. A simple question of temporal quantity: a matter of going a little faster than everyone else. Childhood therefore becomes the privileged site of genius. In Pascal's time, childhood was regarded as a waste of time; the point was to get out of it as fast as possible. Since the romantic era (i.e., since the triumph of the bourgeoisie), it has been a matter of remaining in childhood as long as possible; any adult action imputable to childhood (even to a belated childhood) participates in its intemporality, appears glamorous because produced *in advance.* The *displaced* overvaluation of this age presumes that we regard it as private, closed over itself, possessing a special status, a kind of ineffable and intransmissible essence.

But precisely when childhood is defined as a miracle, we protest that this miracle is nothing other than a premature accession to the adult's powers. Therefore, the specialty of childhood remains ambiguous, tainted with that same ambiguity which affects all the objects of the classical universe: like the green peas in Sartre's comparison, childhood and maturity are different ages, closed, incommunicable, yet identical: the miracle of Minou Drouet is to produce an adult though child's poetry, to have brought the poetic essence into the childhood essence. The astonishment here does not derive from a true destruction of essences (which would be quite healthy), but simply from their hurried amalgam. Which is nicely accounted for by the entirely bourgeois notion of the *child prodigy* (Mozart, Rimbaud, Roberto Benzi); an admirable object insofar as it fulfills the ideal function of all capitalist activity: to gain time, to reduce human duration to a numerative problem of precious moments.

Doubtless, this childhood "essence" has different forms according to the age of its exemplars: for the "modernists," childhood receives its dignity from its very irrationality (at *l'Express,* psychopedagogy has not been overlooked): whence the farcical confusion with Surrealism! But for Monsieur Henriot, who refuses to glorify any source of disorder, childhood must produce nothing except what is charming and distinguished: the child can be neither trivial nor vulgar, which is still to imagine a kind of ideal childhood nature, coming down from heaven outside of any and all social determinism; which is also to leave outside the gate of childhood a great many children, and to recognize as such only the pleasing scions of the bourgeoisie. The age at which man precisely *becomes himself,* i.e., impregnates himself intensely with society and artifice, is paradoxically for Monsieur Henriot the age of "naturalness"; and the age when a child can quite readily kill another child (a news story contemporary with the Minou Drouet case) is, still for Monseiur Henriot, the age when one cannot be lucid and parodic, but only "sincere," "charming," and "distinguished."

Where our commentators find themselves in agreement is with regard to a certain adequate character of Poetry: for them all, Poetry is an uninterrupted series of *finds,* which is the ingenuous name of metaphor. The more stuffed the poem with "formulas," the more it passes for successful. Yet it is only the bad poets who make "good" images, or who at least do only that: they naïvely conceive poetic language as a series of verbal lucky finds added one to the next, convinced no doubt that since poetry is a vehicle of unreality, the object must be *translated* at all costs, turning from Larousse to metaphor, as if it were enough to misname things in order to poeticize them. The result is that this purely metaphoric poetry is entirely built on a sort of poetical dictionary, of which Molière produced several pages for his own day, and in which the poet pursues his poem as if he had to translate "prose" into "verse." The Drouet poetry is, with much application, this uninterrupted metaphor, in which its zealots of both sexes delightedly recognize the bright imperative countenance of Poetry, of *their* Poetry (nothing is more reassuring than a dictionary).

This surplus of "finds" produces its own series of additive admirations; adherence to the poem is no longer a total action, determined slowly and patiently through a period of *rests* (as in music), but an accumulation of ecstasies, of bravos, of salutations addressed to a successful verbal acrobatics: here again, it is quantity which establishes value. Minou Drouet's texts in this sense appear as the antiphrasis of all Poetry insofar as they flee that solitary weapon of writers, literality: yet it is this weapon alone which can strip the poetic metaphor of its artifice, reveal it as the fulguration of a truth, won over a continuous nausea of language. To speak only of modern Poetry (for I doubt that there is an essence of poetry outside of its History)—the poetry of Apollinaire, of course, and not that of Madame Burnat-Provins— it is certain that its beauty, its truth proceed from a profound dialectic between the life and death of language, between the word's density and the weariness of syntax. Now the poetry of Minou Drouet chatters endlessly, like those creatures who are afraid of silence: it visibly dreads the letter and lives on an accumulation of expedients: it identifies life with the fidgets. Which is what reassures us about this poetry. Though some attempt to accuse it of strangeness, though some pretend to receive it with amazement and in a contagion of dithyrambic images, its very garrulity, its procession of "finds," that calculating order of a cheap profusion, all this only establishes a showy and economic Poetry: here again the *simili* reigns, one of the most precious discoveries of the bourgeois world, since it permits making money without diminishing the appearance of the merchandise. It is no accident that *l'Express* has taken over Minou Drouet: hers is the ideal poetry of a universe in which *seeming* is scrupulously calculated; Minou, too, works for others: nothing will do but a little girl in order to accede to the luxury of Poetry.

Such Poetry has of course its Novel, which (in its genre) will be a language quite as neat and practical, as decorative and homely, whose function will be paraded for a reasonable price, a "healthy" novel which will carry in itself the spectacular signs of the fictional, a novel both solid and cheap: the Prix Goncourt, for instance, which was awarded in 1955 as the triumph of the healthy tradition (Stendhal, Balzac, Zola here spell Mozart and Rimbaud) over the decadence of the avant-garde. The important thing, as on the household page of our women's papers, is to be dealing with literary objects whose form, use, and price are quite familiar before we buy them, and that nothing within them should disturb us: for there is no danger in calling Minou Drouet's poetry strange if we recognize it from the first as poetry. Literature, however, only begins in front of the unnamable, facing the perception of an *elsewhere* alien to the very language which seeks it out. It is this creative doubt, this fecund death which our society condemns in its good Literature and exorcises in its bad. To insist at the top of our lungs that the Novel be a novel, that Poetry be poetry and the Theater theater, this sterile tautology is of the same order as the denominative laws which govern, in the Civil Code, the ownership of property: here everything cooperates in the great bourgeois task, which is finally to reduce being to a having, the object to a thing.

After all of which there remains the case of the little girl herself. But let Society not lament over her too hypocritically: it is society which is devouring Minou Drouet, it is of society and society alone that she is the victim. A propitiatory victim sacrificed so the world will be bright, so that poetry, genius, and childhood, in a word *disorder,* will be tamed cheaply, and so that the real rebellion, when it appears, will find its place already taken in the newspapers. Minou Drouet is the child martyr of adults suffering from poetic luxury, she is the kidnap victim of a conformist order which reduces freedom to prodigy status. She is the little girl the beggar pushes onto the sidewalk when back home the mattress is stuffed with money. A little tear for Minou Drouet, a little thrill for poetry, and we are rid of literature.

The
Bourgeois
Art of Song

I T WILL APPEAR IMPERTINENT TO LECTURE AN
excellent baritone, Gérard Souzay, but a release on which
this singer has recorded several of Fauré's songs seems to me
an ideal illustration of a whole musical mythology in which
we can find the principal signs of bourgeois art. This art is
essentially *descriptive,* it constantly imposes not emotion but
the signs of emotion. Which is precisely what Gérard Souzay
does: having to sing, for instance, the words *tristesse affreuse,*
he is not content with the simple semantic content of these
words, nor with the musical line which supports them: he
must further dramatize the phonetics of the *affreux,* must
suspend and then explode the double fricative, releasing misery in the very density of the letters; no one can ignore the
fact that it is a question of particularly terrible pangs. Unfortunately, this pleonasm of intentions muffles both word and
music, and chiefly their junction, which is the very object of
the vocal art. It is true of music as of the other arts, including
literature: the highest form of artistic expression is on the side
of literality, i.e., ultimately of a certain algebra: all form must
tend toward abstraction, which, as we know, is not at all
contrary to sensuality.

And this is precisely what bourgeois art rejects; it always
wants to treat its consumers as naïve customers for whom it
must chew up the work and overindicate the intention, lest
they be insufficiently gripped (but art is also an ambiguity, it
always contradicts, in a sense, its own message, and especially music, which is never, literally, either sad or gay). To

underline the word by the abusive contour of phonetics, to make the guttural of the word *creuse* into the spade digging a grave, and the dental of the word *sein* into a penetrating sweetness, is to practice a literality of intention, not of description, is to establish abusive correspondences. We must remark here, moreover, that the melodramatic spirit which Gérard Souzay's interpretations derive from is precisely one of the historic acquisitions of the bourgeoisie: we rediscover this same overload of intention in the art of our traditional actors, who are, as we know, actors formed by and for the bourgeoisie.

This kind of phonetic pointillism, which gives each letter an incongruous importance, sometimes touches on the absurd: it is a comical solemnity which insists on the double *n* of our *solennel,* and it is a somewhat disgusting happiness, that *bonheur* which is signified by an initial emphasis which expels happiness out of the mouth like a plum pit. Which comes back to a mythological constant, of which we have already spoken apropos of poetry: to conceive of art as an additive series of accumulated, i.e., fully signifying, details: the pointillist perfection of Gérard Souzay is exactly equivalent to Minou Drouet's taste for the metaphor of detail, or to the poultry costumes of *Chantecler* made (in 1910) of thousands of real feathers sewn one over the other. In this art there is an intimidation by detail which is obviously the converse of realism, since realism supposes a typification, i.e., a presence of structure, hence of duration.

This analytic art is doomed to failure particularly in music, whose truth can never be anything but of a respiratory order, prosodic and not phonetic. Hence Gérard Souzay's phrasings are constantly destroyed by the excessive expression of a word, clumsily meant to inject a parasitical intellectual order into the seamless fabric of the song. It seems that we are touching here on a major difficulty of musical execution: to produce the nuance from an internal zone of the music and never impose it from outside as a purely intellective sign: there is a sensual truth of music, a sufficient truth which does not tolerate the constraint of *expression.* This is why the interpretation of excellent virtuosos so often leaves us unsatisfied: their overspectacular *rubato,* product of a visible effort toward signification, destroys an organism which scrupulously contains its own message within itself. Certain amateurs, or better still, certain professionals who have rediscovered what we might call the total letter of the musical text, like Panzéra for song or Lipatti for the piano, manage to add no *intention* to the music: they do not fuss over each detail, contrary to bourgeois art, which is always indiscreet. They trust in the immediately definitive substance of music.

At
the
Music Hall

WHATEVER THE THEATER, WE EXPERIENCE
time there as continuous. Time in the music hall is by
definition interrupted; it is an immediate time. And this is the
meaning of *variety:* that stage time be a just, real, sidereal
time, the time of the thing itself, and not that of its anticipation (tragedy) or of its reconsideration (epic). The advantage
of this literal time is that it can serve gesture best, for it is
quite obvious that gesture exists as spectacle only from the
moment when time is severed (we see this clearly in historical
painting, where the hero's caught gesture, what I have elsewhere called the *numen,* suspends duration). Ultimately, variety is not a simple technique of distraction, but a condition
of artifice (in the Baudelairean sense of the word). To remove
the gesture from its sweetish pulp of duration, to present it
in a superlative, definitive state, to give it the character of
pure visuality, to disengage it from any cause, to exhaust it
as spectacle and not as signification, such is the original
aesthetic of the music hall. Objects (of jugglers) and gestures
(of acrobats), cleansed of time (i.e., of both a pathos and a
logos), gleam like pure artifices, which cannot fail to suggest
the cold precision of Baudelaire's visions of hashish, of a
world absolutely purified of all spirituality because it has,
precisely, renounced time.

Hence everything is done, in the music hall, to prepare a
veritable promotion of object and gesture (which in the
modern West can be done only *against* psychological spectacles, and notably against the theater). A music-hall turn is

almost always constituted by the confrontation of a gesture and a substance: skaters and their lacquered springboard, body exchanges of acrobats, dancers and balancing acts (I confess a great predilection for balancing acts, for in them the body is objectivized *gently:* it is not a hard object catapulted through the air as in pure acrobatics, but rather a soft and dense substance, responsive to very slight movements), comic sculptors and their many-colored clays, prestidigitators gobbling up paper, silk, and cigarettes, pickpockets and their lifted watches, wallets, etc. Now the gesture and its object are the natural raw materials of a value which has had access to the stage only in the music hall (and the circus), and this value is Work. The music hall, at least in its *variety* aspect (for singing, which has become the star of the American version, relates to a different mythology), the music hall is the aesthetic form of work. Here each number is presented either as the exercise or as the product of labor: sometimes the action (that of the juggler, the acrobat, the mime) appears as the *summa* of a long apprenticeship, sometimes the work (artists, sculptors, humorists) is re-created altogether before the public *ab origine.* In any case, it is a new event which is produced, and this event is constituted by the fragile perfection of an effort. Or rather, a more subtle artifice, the effort is perceived at its apogee, at that almost impossible moment when it is about to be engulfed in the perfection of its achievement, without nonetheless having quite abandoned the risk of its failure. At the music hall, everything is *almost* attained, but it is precisely this *almost* which constitutes the spectacle and retains for it, despite its preparation, its virtue as work. Hence what the music-hall spectacle makes visible is not the action's result but its mode of being, the tenuousness of its successful surface. What we have here is a way of making possible a contradictory state of human history: that the artist's gesture should set forth at one and the same time the crude musculature of an arduous labor, standing for the past, and the aerial smoothness of an easy action issuing from a magical heaven: the music hall is human work memorialized and sublimated; danger and effort are signified at the same time that they are subsumed by laughter or by grace.

Naturally the music hall requires a profound enchantment whereby it erases all rugosity from labor and leaves only its finished design. Here reign the gleaming balls, the light wands, the tubular furniture, the chemical silks, the grating chalks, and the glittering clubs; here visual luxury parades *facility,* disposed in the brightness of substances and the continuity of gestures: sometimes man is a support planted in the center, a tree along which slides a woman-branch; sometimes the entire hall shares in the coenesthesia of energy, of weight not vanquished but sublimated by rebounds. In this metallized world, old myths of germination appear and give this representation of labor the guarantee of primordial natural movements, nature always being the image of the continuous, i.e., in the long run, of the easy.

All this muscular magic of the music hall is essentially urban: it is no accident that the music hall is an Anglo-Saxon phenomenon, born in the world of abrupt urban concentrations and the great Protestant myths of labor: the promotion of objects, of metals, and of dreamed gestures, the sublimation of labor by its magical effacement and not by its consecration, as in rural folklore—all this has to do with the artifice of cities. The city rejects the notion of a formless nature, it reduces space to a continuity of solid shiny objects, *products* to which the artist's action gives the glamorous status of a quite human thought: work, especially when mythified, makes matter euphoric because it seems to *think* matter in a spectacular fashion;

metallized, flung away, caught up again, manipulated, quite luminous with movements in perpetual dialogue with gesture, objects lose the sinister stubbornness of their absurdity: artificial and utensile, they cease for a moment to *bore.*

Poujade
and
the Intellectuals

W HO ARE THE INTELLECTUALS, FOR POU-
jade? Essentially "professors" ("Sorbonnards, worthy
pedagogues, county-capital intellectuals") and technicians
("technocrats, polytechnicians, polyvalents or polyvillains").
It is possible that Poujade's severity with regard to intellectuals is based on a simple fiscal rancor: the "professor" is a
profiteer; first of all because he is on salary ("Poor old Pier-
rot, you didn't know how lucky you were when you were on
a salary"*); and then because he doesn't have to declare what
he earns from his private lessons. As for the technician, he's
a sadist: under the loathed form of the comptroller, he tor-
tures the taxpayer. But since Poujadism has sought to construct its major archetypes right away, the intellectual has
quickly been transferred from the fiscal category into that of
the myths.

Like any mythic being, the intellectual participates in a
general theme, a substance: *air,* i.e. (though this is anything
but a scientific identity), *the void.* Superior, the intellectual
soars, he does not "stick" to reality (reality is of course the
ground, an ambiguous myth which signifies at one and the
same time race, rurality, province, good sense, the number-
less obscure, etc.). A restaurant owner who caters regularly
to intellectuals calls them "helicopters," a disparaging image
which subtracts from flight the airplane's virile power: the
intellectual is detached from the real, but remains up in the
air, in place, circling round and round; his ascent is cowardly,

*Most quotations come from Poujade's book *J'ai choisi le combat.*

127

equally remote from the heavens of religion and from the
solid ground of common sense. What he lacks are "roots" in
the nation's heart. The intellectuals are neither idealists nor
realists, they are murky creatures, "dopes." Their exact altitude is that of the *cloud,* an old Aristophanic refrain (the
intellectual, in those days, was Socrates). Suspended in the
upper void, the intellectuals are filled by it, they are "the
drum that resounds in the wind": here we perceive the inevitable basis of all anti-intellectualism: the suspicion of language, the reduction of all adverse speech to a noise, in
accord with the constant procedure of petit-bourgeois polem-
ics, which consists in unmasking in others an infirmity complementary to the one we do not see in ourselves, accusing
the adversary of the effects of our own faults, calling obscurity our own blindness and verbal derangement our own
deafness.

The altitude of "superior" minds is here again identified
with abstraction, doubtless by the intermediary of a state
common to height and to the concept of *rarefaction.* We are
dealing here with a mechanical abstraction, the intellectuals
being merely thinking-machines (what they lack is not
"heart," as the sentimentalist philosophers would say, but
"shrewdness," a kind of tactics nourished by intuition). This
theme of machine-made thought is of course furnished with
picturesque attributes which reinforce its malevolence: first
of all, derision (the intellectuals are skeptical about Poujade),
then malignity, for the machine, in its abstraction, is sadistic:
the officials of the rue de Rivoli are "vicious types" who take
pleasure in making the taxpayer suffer: tools of the System,
they have its cold complexity, that kind of sterile invention,
of negative proliferation which already, apropos of the Jesuits, wrung such loud cries from Michelet. Moreover, the
polytechnicians have, for Poujade, virtually the same role as
the Jesuits for the old liberals: source of all fiscal evils (by the
intermediary of the *rue de Rivoli,* euphemistic designation of

Hell), builders of the System which they subsequently serve like corpses, *perinde ac cadaver,* according to the Jesuit slogan.

This is because science and knowledge, for Poujade, are curiously capable of excess. Since every human phenomenon, even every mental one, exists only in terms of quantity, it suffices to compare its volume to the capacity of the average Poujadist in order to declare it excessive: it is probable that the *excesses* of science are precisely its virtues and that it begins precisely where Poujade finds it to be useless. But this quantification is precious to Poujadist rhetoric, since it engenders monsters, i.e., those polytechnicians who support a pure, abstract science which applies to reality only in a punitive form.

Not that Poujade's judgment of the polytechnicians (and the intellectuals) is hopeless: it will doubtless be possible to "reform" the "French intellectual." What the intellectual suffers from is a hypertrophy (hence he can be operated on); he has added to the small businessman's normal quantity of intelligence an appendage of an excessive weight: this appendage is curiously constituted by science itself, at once objectivized and conceptualized, a kind of ponderous substance which sticks to man or is removed from him exactly like the apple the grocer adds or subtracts in order to obtain an exact weight. That the polytechnician is *besotted by mathematics* means that, once past a certain degree of knowledge, we approach a qualitative world of poisons. Having left behind the healthy limits of quantification, knowledge is discredited insofar as it can no longer be defined as *work.* The intellectuals—polytechnicians, professors, Sorbonnards, and officials—do nothing: they are aesthetes, they frequent not the good country bistro but the *chic bars of the Left Bank.* Here appears a theme dear to all strong regimes: the identification of intellectuality with idleness; the intellectual is by definition lazy, he will have to be put to work once and for all, it will be necessary to convert an activity which can be measured only by its harmful excess into a *concrete* labor, i.e., accessible to Poujadist measurement. We find that ultimately there can be no labor more quantified—and hence more beneficial—than to dig holes or to pile stones: that is labor in the pure state, and moreover it is the labor which all post-Poujadist regimes logically end by reserving for the *idle intellectual.*

This quantification of labor involves, naturally, a promotion of physical strength, that of the muscles, the chest, the arms; conversely, the head is a suspect site insofar as its products are qualitative, not quantitative. Here we return to the usual discredit cast on the brain (*fish rot from the head down,* as Poujade often says), whose fatal disgrace is of course the very eccentricity of its position, right at the top of the body, near the *cloud,* far from the *roots.* We exploit the very ambiguity of *superior* here; a whole cosmogony is constructed which keeps playing on vague similitudes between the physical, the moral, and the social: that the body should struggle against the head is the whole struggle of the *little guys,* of the vital darkness against the up-there.

Poujade himself very rapidly developed the legend of his own physical strength. Furnished with a monitor's diploma, a former RAF flyer, a rugby player, his antecedents warrant his *value:* the chief bestows on his troops, in exchange for their adherence, an essentially measurable strength—after all, it is the *body*'s strength. Hence Poujade's first power (by which we are to understand the basis of the commercial confidence we can place in him) is his resistance ("Poujade is the devil himself, he is unbeatable"). His first campaigns were, above all, physical performances which touched on the superhuman ("He's the devil in person"). This steely strength produces ubiquity (Poujade is everywhere at once), it affects matter itself (Poujade cracks up all the cars he uses).

Yet there is another value in Poujade besides resistance: a kind of physical *charm,* lavished over and above his strength-as-merchandise, like one of those superfluous objects by which, in archaic law, the acquirer bound the vendor of real estate: this "tip" which establishes the leader and appears as Poujade's genius, the share set aside for quality in this economy of pure computation, is *his voice.* Doubtless, it has issued from a privileged site of the body, a site at once median and muscular, the thorax, which is in all this corporeal mythology the anti-head *par excellence;* but the voice, vehicle of the correcting word, escapes the harsh law of quantities: for the process of wear and tear, the fate of ordinary objects, it substitutes its fragility, a glorious risk of deluxe objects; for it, we invoke not the heroic scorn of fatigue, not implacable endurance, but rather the delicate caress of the vaporizer, the velvety support of the microphone; Poujade's voice receives by transference the imponderable and glamorous value devolved, in other mythologies, upon the intellectual's brain.

Naturally, Poujade's lieutenants must participate in the same image, cruder, less diabolic, of course—that of the "stalwart." "Virile Launay, former rugby player . . . with his powerful hairy forearms . . . doesn't look like an *enfant de Marie.*" Cantalou, "tall, powerful, muscular, has a clear gaze, and a frank, virile handshake." For, according to a familiar crasis, physical plenitude establishes a kind of moral clarity: only the strong can be frank. As we can imagine, the essence common to all these powers is virility, for which the moral substitute is "character," a rival of the intelligence, which is not admitted into the Poujadist heaven: it is replaced by a special intellectual virtue: *shrewdness;* the hero, for Poujade, is a being endowed with both aggressiveness and cunning. This perspicuity, however intellective it may be, does not reintroduce reason, abhorred in the Poujadist pantheon: the petit-bourgeois gods grant or withdraw it at will, according to a pure order of *chance:* it is, moreover, all things considered, a virtually physical gift, comparable to an animal's sense of smell; merely a rare flower of strength, an entirely nervous power of sensing what is in the wind ("Me, I walk by radar").

Conversely, it is through his corporeal mediocrity that the intellectual is condemned: Mendès-France looks like "a bottle of Vichy water" (double scorn, addressed to water and to dyspepsia). Sheltering in the hypertrophy of a fragile and useless head, the entire intellectual being is stricken by the gravest of physical flaws, *fatigue* (corporeal substitute for decadence): though idle, he is congenitally exhausted, just as the Poujadist, though hard-working, is always fresh and ready. We touch here upon the profound idea of any morality of the human body: the idea of race. The intellectuals are one race, the Poujadists are another.

Yet Poujade has a conception of race that at first glance is paradoxical. Remarking that the average Frenchman is the product of many mixtures (the familiar refrain: France, the racial melting pot), it is this variety of origins which Poujade contrasts proudly with the narrow sect of those who have never mixed their blood with any but each other (by which is meant, of course, the Jews). He exclaims, pointing to Mendès-France: "You're the racist!"; then he explains: "Of the two of us, he's the one who can be a racist, he's the one who has a race." Poujade practices what we might call the racism of cross-breeding, without danger, moreover, since the vaunted "cross-breeding" has never mixed, according to Poujade himself, anything but Duponts, Durands, and Poujades, i.e., the same with the same. Obviously the notion of a synthetic "race" is a precious one, for it permits playing sometimes on syncretism, sometimes on race. In the first case, Poujade uses the old, once-revolutionary notion of the Nation, which has nourished all the French liberalisms (Michelet vs. Augustin Thierry, Gide vs. Barrès, etc.): "My ancestors, Celts, Gauls, everything else all mixed together. I

am the fruit of the melting pot of invasions and exoduses."
In the second case, he rediscovers with no difficulty at all the
fundamental racist object, Blood (here it is chiefly Celtic
blood, that of Le Pen, *solid Breton,* separated by a racial
abyss from the *aesthetes of the New Left,* or Gallic blood in
which Mendès is lacking). As for the intelligence, we are
dealing here with an arbitrary distribution of values: the
addition of certain bloods (that of the Duponts, the Durands,
and the Poujades) produces only pure blood, and we may
remain within the reassuring order of a summation of homogeneous quantities; but other bloods (that, notably, of the
technocrats without a country) are purely qualificational
phenomena, thereby discredited in the Poujadist universe;
they cannot interbreed, accede to the salvation of the large
French quantity, to that "vulgar" whose numerical triumph
is opposed to the fatigue of "distinguished" intellectuals.

This racial opposition between the strong and the exhausted, the Gauls and the men without a country, the vulgar
and the distinguished, is, moreover, quite simply the opposition between the province and Paris. Paris summarizes all the
French vices: System, sadism, intellectuality, fatigue: "Paris
is a monster, for life there is unbalanced: life shakes you up,
dazzles and overwhelms you from morning to night, etc."
Paris participates in that same poison, an essentially qualitative substance (what Poujade elsewhere calls, not realizing
how well he is putting it: dialectics), which as we have seen
is opposed to the quantitative world of good sense. To confront "quality" was for Poujade the decisive test, his Rubi-
con: *to go up to Paris,* to collect there the moderate provincial
deputies corrupted by the capital, veritable renegades of their
race, waited for back home in the village with pitchforks—
this expedition has defined a great racial migration even more
than a political extension.

Confronting so constant a suspicion, could Poujade rescue
some form of the intellectual, give him an ideal image, in a

133

word postulate a *Poujadist intellectual?* Poujade merely tells us that only "intellectuals worthy of the name" will enter his Olympus. Thus we are back to one of these famous definitions by identity (A = A), which I have on several occasions called tautologies, i.e., nothingness. All anti-intellectualism ends this way in the death of language, i.e., in the destruction of sociability.

Most of these Poujadist themes, paradoxical as it may appear, are corruptions of romantic themes. When Poujade wants to define the People, it is the preface to *Ruy Blas* that he quotes at length: and the intellectual seen by Poujade is more or less Michelet's jurist and Jesuit, dry, empty, sterile, and sneering. This is because today's petite bourgeoisie is reaping the ideological heritage of yesterday's liberal bourgeoisie, precisely the one which assisted its social promotion: Michelet's sentimentalism contained many reactionary seeds. As Barrès knew. If it were not for all the discrepancies of talent, Poujade could still sign many pages of Michelet's *Le Peuple* (1846).

Which is why, precisely on this matter of the intellectuals, Poujadism goes much further than Poujade; the anti-intellectualist ideology affects various political milieux, and it is not necessary to be a Poujadist to nourish a hatred of ideas. For what is inculpated here is any form of explicative, committed culture, and what is saved is an "innocent" culture, the culture whose naïveté leaves the tyrant's hands free. This is why writers in the literal sense of the word are not excluded by the Poujadist family (some, extremely well known at that, have sent their works to Poujade embellished with flattering dedications). What is condemned is the intellectual, i.e., a consciousness, or better still: an Observation (Poujade recalls somewhere how much, as a *lycée* student, he suffered from being looked at by his fellow students). *That no one look at us* is the principle of Poujadist anti-intellectualism. Only, from the ethnologist's point of view, the practices of integration and of exclusion are obviously complementary, and in a sense which is not the one he supposes, Poujade needs intellectuals, for if he condemns them it is on account of a magical evil: in the Poujadist society, the intellectual has the accursed and necessary role of a lapsed witch doctor.

The
Two
Salons

THE ANCIENT EGYPTIANS, IT IS SAID, IN-
scribed their temples within a symbolic space corresponding to the figure of a human body. Similarly the Salon
of Office Equipment, lodged under the huge shell of La Défense, is our whole brain: here the functions of memory (filing
systems), there those of written language (typewriters) or of
spoken language (dictaphones), and over there the motor
functions (classification and transfer of orders). This Salon is
much more civilized than its triumphant rival, the Auto
Salon. At the Grand Palais, we see a variety of models of one
and the same object: the only relation among these variations
is that of competition; at La Défense, on the contrary, not
only do the objects differ, but they complement each other as
well, they participate in an economy of the mind. The Auto
Salon is a fair, in the almost ritual sense of the word; the
Office Equipment Salon is a little cosmography, the representation of a structure.

The Automobile is an object of leisure, it gives rise to
activities of satisfaction, not of conquest; its technological
development no longer corresponds to a new labor of the
intelligence. Whatever its popular successes, the Automobile participates in a myth already satiated, the myth of
the Mechanical. Now, what the Office Salon suggests is
that this myth is undergoing a transformation. For a very
long time, in mythic terms, the machine has been a collection of gears, i.e., of relays; its course was symbolically

that of a twisted but on the whole linear causality: you put some liquid in here and it came out of the movement there; from wheel to wheel, from lever to lever, a stubborn impulse circulated, almost conscious of its goal; and it is this very trajectory which absorbed amazement, i.e., myth. Today the mythic accent is no longer put on a trajectory but on a distribution: paradoxically, the cybernetic imagination revives the notion of the human brain; proposes, within the machine, the spectacle of an *organization,* i.e., of an intelligence, i.e., of a quality. We might say that the time has come (I am speaking of course only of mythic, not social data) when the machine no longer mechanizes man, when it is man who humanizes the machine by imposing upon it the structure of his own brain.*

The very publicity for the Office Salon, whose prestige has grown from year to year, sufficiently attests that our century is no longer that of the mechanical. Of course, machines abound in this Salon; but they no longer raise problems, they are no longer the object of language (of amazement), they are language itself, i.e., they are already insignificant, entirely dissolved into usage. Equipment here is no longer anything but a commercial notion; the myth, the spectacle, is *organization.* Articles are sold, but what we look at is a complex substance, consisting of objects, gestures, and time, and this substance is manipulated, distributed according to a Reason: this is not a Salon of Techniques, but of Structures, and that is why this Salon, much more than that of the Auto, is an avant-garde phenomenon: its real life is not on the level of some new and miraculous machine which causes a sensation (the age of gadgets is just about past), it is in that *elegant* effort (in

---

*Which is why any contestation of the machine in the name of humanism seems to me a complete misunderstanding of the development of our modern society.

the mathematical sense of the adjective) of the human intelligence *to begin reality over again* according to the
order of men and not according to the order of things.

In its heroic period, the machine was the spectacle of
an effect miraculously removed from its cause; here, on
the contrary, it is no longer a product which is treated, it
is a whole topological ensemble of gestures and informa-
tion, of which the Salon itself, in its material enclosure,
from the dictaphone department to that of retrieval systems, represents the gigantic memory. For the problem
raised here is the very one whose solution dominates any
subjection of nature: how on one hand to form a complete
inventory, vaster than could ever have been hoped, of the
entire knowledge of an undertaking, and how on the other
hand to extract from this reservoir the very element
needed? How to construct that philosophic pyramid of
which the base is knowledge and the summit action? To
inscribe, then to call up, to undo the very number one has
constituted, in favor of the singular—that is a new movement which is no longer, strictly speaking, one of transformation but rather of disposition: the myth of the substantial transmutations of matter, which has tormented
the West from alchemy to atomic physics, gives way to a
new imagination: the notion that the very *classification* of
the universe is the material act by which man appropri-
ates that universe. Against or at least after the romantic
image of a unique substance which was to be *varied* without ever losing its relations, it is now the discontinuous
which is the motor image of human research: to distin-
guish, to compare, to cite, to reject, these are today *universal* operations, no longer destined, as they were for
centuries, to tranquilize the mind, to feed it reassuring ali-

bis, but to modify reality in terms of technology. Whereas
society, regarding any analytical activity with suspicion, is
still kept imprisoned within a whole anti-intellectualist
mythology, it is precisely the intellectual act *par excellence,* the *distinguo,* which marks out an entire new research, from cybernetic machines to the planning of the
technocrats, a value henceforth common to all systems, to
all labors: having descended from its ancient theological
heavens, scholasticism, applied to reality, becomes progressive once again.

Dining
Car

WHAT COMPAGNIE COOK'S *PRIX-FIXE* SUP-
plies is not so much food as a philosophy. Its principle is a wager: that the traveler should consume at the
very heart of his journey everything constitutively opposed
by the journey. Hence the first goal is to purify the meal
of any strictly nutritive finality, to conceal by a protocol
of attentions its very contingency, which is quite simply to
eat on a train. Each constraint seems to produce its contrary freedom, each gesture is a denial of its original limits. For example, the very lack of room engenders a great
deal of napery, a cloud of tablecloths and napkins (they're
wrapped around everything, even the breadbasket), many
covers—as if neither space nor time were in short supply
for storing and washing them.

Beyond this profusion, a whole mirage of solidity is proposed: starched linen, massive flatware, everything here thea-
trically tends to exceed mere utensility, attesting that we are
still within a civilization of the *simili* (whose origin Sombart
has located at the first stage of capitalism), whereas, for
example, in American life, the object's goal is its swift destruction, its materiality must not survive its use, where-unto
it is delicately and furiously manufactured out of paper. In
the Cook version of luxury, on the contrary, the massiveness
of the objects always suggests that despite certain special
characteristics of travel (singularity, anonymity), they have
just been removed from some rich cupboard, whose roots—

as in the remotest parts of our countryside—reach deep into the ground.

The house may be evoked, yet its theme is eluded, distorted, in favor of its mythic substitute, the luxury restaurant; though the journey is destroyed or at least sublimated, it is not the *home* which is recuperated here, but the special occasion, "eating out," Sunday best . . . The household, the kitchen are taken over by men of art and skill, whose menu furnishes us with their respectable names (Captain Bérard, Chef Couty); we are to consume the products of a responsible artisanry: everything here must triumph over the natural anonymity of a food factory. Of course the menu obeys the law of overnomination which defines luxury cuisine; the dishes have names all the more glamorous in that they emerge from an invisible galley, accompany suburbs and shipping stations; this is the triumph of freedom over necessity: what could be more glorious than to be eating filets of sole Bagratian while riding through Laroche-Migennes? Here, nothing is without a name: boiling in water inevitably becomes *meunière,* frying *cocotte,* thickened soup *crème portugaise.* Further, what is functionally no more than a piece of meat served with vegetables is emphatically coined as three distinct names, for among us Frenchmen, *petit-bourgeois* luxury is always plural (in lower-class restaurants, on the contrary, the dish concentrates its name in the meat, the vegetables are only a "garnish"). The problem here is to elude contingency—that of the journey, that of the food: Cook's style is a variety of the baroque genre, a representation of uselessness.

But what constitutes the specialty of the dining car is that this *disinterested* universe, whose entire pomp aims at modestly liquidating the trivial motives of "eating," is surreptitiously undermined by the very contingency which it claimed to expel, so that the theater where we experience it is a mixture of rhetoric and naturalism, of emphatic luxury and inevitable planning, of art and technology: in short, number maliciously recuperates the individual. The traveler is subjected to a fatal rhythm of consumption, whose unit is the *wave:* first sign of an intensive functionalization, all the operations of the service are decomposed, none can begin until the last is exhausted, the meal is merely a series of discontinuous takes: we ingest, we wait, like ruminants in their stalls, passively fed according to a series of mouthfuls which sweating keepers busily and fairly distribute down a long service corridor. There are thirteen waves: the apéritifs, the drink orders, the uncorking of the bottles, the five courses, the second bread (this one, stale and plebeian, contrasts pitifully with the inaugural roll), coffee, liqueurs, the bill, payment. The process is an inflexible one, so that this whole décor of leisure ends by manifesting what it graciously claimed to sublimate: the methodical filling of stomachs. Everything down to the merest internal protocols helps restore to these splendid exotic names their banally nutritional content: the sole Bagratian, the roast chicken with mushrooms and endive *meunière* are reduced to the anonymous rank of ready-made *portions:* the nobly circular gesture with which the server extracts each of them from its alignment, pretending to choose the best piece with a profound scoop of his spoon but coming up, after all, with nothing better than the next in the row—this anthological gesture does not succeed in reconverting the *ration* into a dish: thus, despite its festive name, the *bombe glacèe* manifests itself essentially as the object of a *delivery:* the knife is inserted, the slice falls onto the spatula, the spatula moves over your plate, drops its contents, then the cycle begins all over again according to the best techniques of certain drilling and conveying apparatus.

In short, what is surprising, in Cook's cycle, is this Sisyphean effort to cover with a disinterested veil the implacable materiality of *eating-while-traveling,* that bizarre collusion between the geometrism of (spatial and scheduling) constraints and the rhetoric of the presentation. But it is probably the very spectacle of this effort that we are paying for: Cook gives us a rudiment of dialectics, the proof of a contradiction in which our journey is denied without ceasing to be perceived: the meal occurs at the heart of a movement, the landscape slides along motionless panes of glass, it becomes a fleeting accessory of the alimentary protocol; by food, we participate in a transported immobility. Thus each time man constructs his displacement, it is to give it the superstructure of a house; each time he detaches himself from the ground, he requires its guarantee: all the *arts* of travel have for their goal the very illusion of immobility: in the panic and pleasure of transplantation, Cook sells the spectacle of a stability.

Cottage
Industry

HAVING FOUNDED *LA MAISON DU SOLDAT* AS well as an employment agency, *Tricots à domicile* (Knitting at home), General Massu's wife conducts a tireless campaign on the social front as well. According to *Aux Ecoutes* (March 13, 1959), her headquarters in the rue d'Isly, in Algiers, is as stark as a warrior's tent; such asceticism offers a lesson to the Administration's futile proliferation of paperwork; but above all, in the image of those great scientists who pick up a piece of chalk and put the universe into an equation, or like the true masters of the world, who think in front of a bare desk, Mme la Générale signifies by the choice of this austere décor that the instruments of action are trivial, that only the brain matters, that profound thoughts are intangible, that a great captain does without the insignia of his function, as a great doctor makes his calls without a white gown or a great professor gives his lectures without notes—in short, that abstraction is the only substance worthy of genius: the nakedness of the premises guarantees that what is dealt with there is essential.

In this rarefied and anonymous space, only two objects link Mme la Générale to the world, like the two terms of a circuit of which she is but the modest relay: a few close-ups of General Massu in paratrooper's uniform, from which she doubtless receives an inspiring influx; and at the other end, signs of the quite earthly substance which must be stirred, transformed, two telephones which ring constantly, informing Mme la Générale minute by minute of the successive episodes of the Knitting Campaign. For this almost abstract site is also an ubiquitarian one: on it everything converges, from it everything radiates, a single mind generates multiple effects, since there are *two* telephones. In the fashion of every great strategist, Mme la Générale copes (we are told), which means she serves on several fronts at once—here the defeatist press, there the *fellagha;* whence the plurality of weapons, yesterday sewing machines, today *tricots à domicile.* Yet this entirely contingent activity is subject to a great military philosophy. The Good Soldier knows how to conquer, the Great Captain does better, he decides as to the essence of things. The philosophy of Madame la Générale Massu is resolutely nominalist. When will the war in Algeria end? *The day when no one in France says it cannot be settled.* In short, things exist only because we name them; therefore, according to the venerable magic procedure, we suppress the name and thereby suppress the thing. Madame la Générale dreams of a great silent France where no one speaks of anything but knitting.

Madame la Générale has one sovereign attribute of the Great Captain: *smiling calm.* How many things are signified by this tranquil smile of the Soldier! The certainty of the Cause and the excellence of its ways; the superhumanity of an organism which remains master of itself and the universe despite two simultaneous telephones; a certain earthly "absence," the discreet reflection of a privileged communication with the gods, the dreamy sentiment that the Knitting Front is merely, in spite of everything, mundane; a magnanimous indulgence for an all-too-human agitation partaken only to be sublimated; the *askesis* of all hatred, the serenity of the Stoic; finally, perhaps, and above all, the privilege of the Sex, whose vocation is to illuminate with a smile the fierce battles men, those big Babies, wage against each other; a sibylline goddess on Olympus, Madame la Générale inflects her calm smile with the wisdom of *One Who Knows* (but does not tell) *All,* for to smile is always to keep something back.

Of course Madame la Générale implicitly recognizes that not everything is for the best in Algeria. Otherwise, would she have founded *Tricots à domicile?* But the evil is limited, we learn—the evil is the Moslem woman's idleness and consequent poverty, to remedy which 15,000 francs a month will suffice (the remuneration provided by *Tricots à domicile*), and something to do around the house. Thus General Massu and Madame la Générale, by a healthy division of functions, can handle the complementary aspects of the Algerian "problem": as a man, the General wages war, reduces the *fellagha;* as a woman, Mme la Générale reconstructs, rallies the feminine populations by having them knit at home.

Here two themes of different origin combine. The first, that of a cottage industry, defines one of the most obsolete forms of capitalist alienation: Madame Massu's program dates back to the Restoration. But above all—to remain within the limits of mythological analysis—this form of wage earning is decked out with a triple morality: first, bringing the job to the labor force endows it with a certain spirituality, opposes the factory's inhumanity by the *enriching* virtues of natural labor and a quasi-Biblical style; then, work at home preserves the couple, appears to emancipate the wife, to grant her the masculine privilege of earning, without having to abandon her pots and her laundry, i.e., what is nobly called *the hearth;* and finally, according to the fundamental sophism of bourgeois ideology, we cunningly give charity the aspect of labor, saving both our soul and the laws of economics; alms sublimates work, work masks alms; in short, we kill two birds with one stone, which is the golden rule of a bookkeeping civilization. *Aux Écoutes* has been kind enough to decompose the two phases of this precious swivel: Monseigneur Duval's vicar having presented Mme Massu, "at the moment of the battle of Algiers," with a suitcase containing fifty million francs on behalf of some anonymous penitent (but improbably a *fellah*), the journalist does not fail to put this fabulous alms into a fatal relation with the organizations of solidarity Mme la Générale has created: from charity to employment agency, the way is straight and smooth.

The second theme which looms up behind Mme Massu's *organization* is that of the Moslem Woman. This Moslem Woman, whom we have heard so much about since May 13 —for she has been filmed for us, always veiled but voting with determination, a delicate marriage between local color and political integration—is a touching, chaste, in short harmless substitute for the proletariat. Named, acknowledged, the existence of an Algerian proletariat would demand projects of reform, even of revolution, in any case, to say the least, an empirical improvement of its real status. With the Moslem Woman, no such risk: we can remain within morality, can nobly favor an *evolution,* can rediscover the nonchalant rhythm of civilized progress. But above all, this diversionary operation affects the very cause of the Algerian evil: to claim, in a Moslem country, to liberate its women is surreptitiously to transform the colonial responsibility into an Islamic one, for it suggests that the Moslem Woman is retarded because she is subject to a religion it is well known she subserves; hence it appears that we can embark all of colonialism on the rotten ship of religious obscurantism, implicitly questioning a retrograde dogma without, for all that, abandoning the alibi of a "different civilization" whose substantial exoticism (native in a *gandourah* standing in front of an oil well, black man in a loincloth knocking down from the fruit trees "the wealth of the tropics") is necessary to France's ecumenicism. Islam provides at one and the same time a motive of easy emulation and a distracting décor: we integrate these women without unveiling them.

Buffet
Finishes Off
New York

BERNARD BUFFET'S NEW YORK WILL NOT UN-
settle many prejudices: it is a city of geometric heights,
a petrified desert of grids and lattices, an inferno of greenish
abstraction under a flat sky, a real Metropolis from which
man is absent by his very accumulation; the implicit morality
of our new Greuze is that we are distinctly happier in Belle-
ville than in Manhattan. This is a folklore New York rather
like Bizet's Spain or the Italy of the Théâtre Mogador: an
exoticism which confirms the Frenchman in the excellence of
his habitat.

According to Buffet, the architecture of this city is uniformly longiform and quadrangular. Here the grid reigns
under its most ill-favored aspect: the contour, this black line
which encloses everything, obviously intends to expel man
from the city. By obsessively multiplying the window, by
inlaying it with black, Buffet empties it, destroys it, makes the
living edifice into a dead surface, as if number, unless it is
swarming, must fatally establish an abstract order; Buffet
geometrizes New York the better to depopulate it: everyone
knows that abstraction is "sterile." Now, to my sense of it,
one of the lessons of this marvelous city is that abstraction
is alive, and it must paradoxically be a painter who denies us
this truth. But no doubt only an "abstract" painter could do
justice to New York, could understand that planes and lines,
form and meaning are as intensely alive here as in one of
Mondrian's compositions: here figuration cunningly serves to

149

destroy: to paint is to deceive. Buffet has "figured" New York in order to get rid of it.

The same aggression is to be noted with regard to the city's great commonplace, the skyscraper. What is astonishing about the skyscraper is that it does not astonish. When we actually see one (but do we ever see one, actually?), the feeling it inspires is: *why not?* For Buffet, on the contrary, the skyscraper always seems to remain in an anthological state, and this is always what he presents, refining on the needle, that obsessive shape of his thin and angular style. As if his very canvas, in its material proportions, *makes* the sky-scraper; for him the skyscraper is a Being, and a prejudged one. Of course Buffet is sometimes sensitive to the city's magnificent *breadth,* to the scope of its *base* (for New York is a splendidly *set* city, like all fabulous metropolises); hence he paints a veritable façade of structures, he sees New York full-face, which is a good way of freeing himself from it, or he suspends the great scroll of a bridge in his foreground; but even in these efforts at enlargement, height surreptitiously reappears: the panorama spreads out the skyscrapers only to profile them in a jerky succession, the bridge dominates them only to manifest their aggressive vigor in the distance. There is a mythic combat here between *the Base and the Summit,* as Char says; but instead of altitude being absorbed in the foreground mass (for New York is in fact a deep city, not a high one), Buffet bequeaths it his absurd solitude; he paints the skyscrapers as if they were empty cathedrals: he flattens the "landscape."

Buffet finishes off New York by depopulating the streets. I am not saying that the truth of New York is a *swarm,* which is a Neapolitan, a European notion. Urbanism itself, this checkerboard of nameless streets, is the price that has to be paid in order that the streets be useful and no longer pictur-esque, in order that men and objects circulate, adapt them-selves to the distances, rule effectively over this enormous urban nature: the biggest city in the world (with Tokyo) is also the one we possess in an afternoon, by the most exciting of operations, since here *to possess* is *to understand:* New York exposes itself to intellection, and our familiarity with it comes very quickly. This is the purpose of these numbered streets, inflexibly distributed according to regular distances: not to make the city into a huge machine and man into an automaton, as we are repeatedly and stupidly told by those for whom tortuosity and dirt are the gauges of spirituality, but on the contrary to master the distances and orientations by the mind, to put at one man's disposal the space of these twelve million, this fabulous reservoir, this world emporium in which *all* goods exist except the metaphysical variety. This is the purpose of New York's geometry: that each individual should be *poetically* the owner of the capital of the world. It is not up, toward the sky, that you must look in New York; it is down, toward men and merchandise: by an admirable static paradox, the skyscraper establishes the block, the block creates the street, the street offers itself to man. Buffet of course proceeds in the opposite direction: he empties the street, climbs up the façades, grazes the surfaces, he rarefies: his New York is an anti-city.

To paint New York from above, at the top, is to rely once again on the first spiritualist myth, i.e., that geometry kills man. In his way, Buffet follows in the wake of our venerable moralists, for whom the refrigerator is antipathetic to the soul. The intentional desolation of his New York—what can it mean except that it is bad for man to live in groups, that number kills the spirit, that too many bathrooms are harmful to the spiritual health of a nation, that a world that is too "modern" is a sinister world, that we are bored when we are comfortable, in short, according to the most reactionary remark of human history, the alibi of all exploitations, that "money doesn't make happiness"? Myself, I can readily imagine that working in New York is a terrible thing, but it is not New York which is terrible, it is work. By making this city into a petrified, infantile necropolis looming up out of an "abstract" age (but not, alas! out of an abstract art), Buffet once again diverts history into metaphysics. Black looks at America always begin with the skyscrapers, and stick there. Yet what the Pilgrims unloaded from the *Mayflower* was not only empiricism, the spirit of enterprise, in short the seed which has doubtless produced the most stupendous city in the world, but also Puritanism and profit, money and metaphysics. What is good, Buffet discredits. And what is bad, he passes over in silence.